JUL - - 2007

SCULPTURE

by Don Nardo

LUCENT BOOKS

An imprint of Thomson Gale, a part of The Thomson Corporation

Detroit • New York • San Francisco • San Diego • New Haven, Conn.
Waterville, Maine • London • Munich

THOMSON

™

GALE

© 2007 Thomson Gale, a part of The Thomson Corporation.

Thomson and Star Logo are trademarks and Gale and Lucent Books are registered trademarks used herein under license.

For more information, contact
Lucent Books
27500 Drake Rd.
Farmington Hills, MI 48331-3535
Or you can visit our Internet site at http://www.gale.com

LIBRARY OF CONGRESS CATALOGING-IN-PUBLICATION DATA

Nardo, Don, 1947–
    Sculpture / by Don Nardo.
        p. cm. — (Eye on art)
    Includes bibliographical references and index.
        ISBN 1-59018-966-3 (hard cover : alk. paper) 1. Sculpture—History.
    I. Title. II. Series
        NB60.N37 2006
        730.9—dc22   2006012609

Printed in the United States of America

CONTENTS

Foreword

"Art has no other purpose than to brush aside . . . everything that veils reality from us in order to bring us face to face with reality itself."

—French philosopher Henri-Louis Bergson

Some thirty-one thousand years ago, early humans painted strikingly sophisticated images of horses, bison, rhinoceroses, bears, and other animals on the walls of a cave in southern France. The meaning of these elaborate pictures is unknown, although some experts speculate that they held ceremonial significance. Regardless of their intended purpose, the Chauvet-Pont-d'Arc cave paintings represent some of the first known expressions of the artistic impulse.

From the Paleolithic era to the present day, human beings have continued to create works of visual art. Artists have developed painting, drawing, sculpture, engraving, and many other techniques to produce visual representations of landscapes, the human form, religious and historical events, and countless other subjects. The artistic impulse also finds expression in glass, jewelry, and new forms inspired by new technology. Indeed, judging by humanity's prolific artistic output throughout history, one must conclude that the compulsion to produce art is an inherent aspect of being human, and the results are among humanity's greatest cultural achievements: masterpieces such as the architectural marvels of ancient Greece, Michelangelo's perfectly rendered statue *David*, Vincent van Gogh's visionary painting *Starry Night*, and endless other treasures.

The creative impulse serves many purposes for society. At its most basic level, art is a form of entertainment or the means for a satisfying or pleasant aesthetic experience. But art's true power lies not in its potential to entertain and delight but in its ability to enlighten, to reveal the truth, and by doing so to uplift the human spirit and transform the human race.

One of the primary functions of art has been to serve religion. For most of Western history, for example, artists were paid by the church to produce works with religious themes and subjects. Art was thus a tool to help human beings transcend mundane, secular reality and achieve spiritual enlightenment. One of the best-known, and largest-scale, examples of Christian religious art is the Sistine Chapel in the Vatican in Rome. In 1508 Pope Julius II commissioned Italian Renaissance artist Michelangelo to paint the chapel's vaulted ceiling, an area of 640 square yards (535 sq. m.). Michelangelo spent four years on scaffolding, his neck craned, creating a panoramic fresco of some three hundred human figures. His paintings depict Old Testament prophets and heroes, sibyls of Greek mythology, and nine scenes from the Book of Genesis, including the Creation of Adam, the Fall of Adam and Eve from the Garden of Eden, and the Flood. The ceiling of the Sistine Chapel is considered one of the greatest works of Western art and has inspired the awe of countless Christian pilgrims and other religious seekers. As eighteenth-century German poet and author Johann Wolfgang von Goethe wrote, "Until you have seen this Sistine Chapel, you can have no adequate conception of what man is capable of."

In addition to inspiring religious fervor, art can serve as a force for social change. Artists are among the visionaries of any culture. As such, they often perceive injustice and wrongdoing and confront others by reflecting what they see in their work. One classic example of art as social commentary was created in May 1937, during the brutal Spanish civil war. On May 1 Spanish artist Pablo Picasso learned of the recent attack on the small Basque village of Guernica by German airplanes allied with fascist forces led by Francisco Franco. The German pilots had used the village for target practice, a three-hour bombing that killed sixteen hundred civilians. Picasso, living in Paris, channeled his outrage over the massacre into his painting *Guernica*, a black, white, and gray mural that depicts dismembered animals and fractured human figures whose faces are contorted in agonized expressions. Initially, critics and the public condemned the painting as an incoherent hodgepodge, but the work soon came to be seen as a powerful antiwar statement and remains an iconic symbol of the violence and terror that dominated world events during the remainder of the twentieth century.

The impulse to create art—whether painting animals with crude pigments on a cave wall, sculpting a human form from marble, or commemorating human tragedy in a mural—thus serves many purposes. It offers an entertaining diversion, nourishes the imagination and the spirit, decorates and beautifies the world, and chronicles the age. But underlying all these functions is the desire to reveal that which is obscure—to illuminate, clarify, and perhaps ennoble. As Picasso himself stated, "The purpose of art is washing the dust of daily life off our souls."

The Eye on Art series is intended to assist readers in understanding the various roles of art in society. Each volume offers an in-depth exploration of a major artistic movement, medium, figure, or profession. All books in the series are beautifully illustrated with full-color photographs and diagrams. Riveting narrative, clear technical explanation, informative sidebars, fully documented quotes, a bibliography, and a thorough index all provide excellent starting points for research and discussion. With these features, the Eye on Art series is a useful introduction to the world of art—a world that can offer both insight and inspiration.

Beyond Illusion: Sculpture as an Interactive Art

Sculpture is one of the oldest arts invented and practiced by humans. It likely ranks with storytelling, dancing, and painting as one of the four earliest forms of artistic expression that appeared in what modern scholars call the Stone Age—the long era in which people used tools and weapons made of stone. Other arts, including architecture, ceramics, and playing musical instruments, likely came later.

These and other categories of art were and remain general. Each breaks down into several different styles, approaches, and techniques. For example, paintings have been executed in styles ranging from realistic to impressionistic and abstract. Some have been done on walls; others on canvas; and still others on pottery, wood, cloth, and other materials. Paint has been applied using brushes, sponges, spray devices, and even the hands. In addition, paints have been manufactured from a wide range of minerals, liquids, and other substances.

Similarly, over time sculptors have devised a number of diverse styles and techniques. One common style of or approach to sculpture is called relief. A relief is a sculpted image or scene in which the figures or objects depicted are raised from, but still attached to, a flat surface. A widely familiar example consists of the human faces and heads on coins.

The faces are raised slightly from the flat backgrounds. Such reliefs that feature a minimal amount of extension into three-dimensional space are often referred to as bas-reliefs, meaning low reliefs. Reliefs in which the figures or objects extend more fully into three-dimensional space are said to be alto-reliefs, meaning high reliefs. The faces of four U.S. presidents projecting from the rocky summit of Mount Rushmore in South Dakota are famous examples. Sculptors also create works in which the figures or objects break free of the background and exist completely in three dimensions. Such sculptures, including statues and figurines, are said to be freestanding.

Sculptures can also be produced in a number of different ways, that is, using various sculpting techniques. In one common technique, called modeling, the artist molds a soft substance such as clay or wax into the desired shape using his or her hands or one or more of a wide range of tools. The molded image then dries into a hardened state. It might then be baked in an oven to make it more durable, or it might be used

Mount Rushmore National Monument, one of the largest relief sculptures in the world, was completed in 1941 by sculptor Gutzon Borglum.

to make hollow casts into which the sculptor pours liquid metal or glass. This is how the 5-ton (4.5 metric tons) bronze statue of Thomas Jefferson, created for the Jefferson Memorial in Washington, D.C., by sculptor Rudolph Evans, was cast. A second major sculpting technique, carving, involves the chipping away of some hard material, often stone, to produce the desired three-dimensional image. Some famous and magnificent examples are the *David* and *Pietà* of the Italian Renaissance master Michelangelo Buonarroti.

Realism Through Depth

Whatever styles or techniques sculptors may choose to execute their works, these works all share certain distinctive qualities that differentiate them from works produced in other artistic mediums. Chief among these qualities is the achievement of realism through depth. In other words, a sculptor exploits the three-dimensional aspects of his or her art at least in part to echo, or mirror, real life. Painting also attempts to mirror or capture real life. However, painters do this in two dimensions, on a flat surface, by using subtle gradations of light and dark pigments to create the illusion of depth. By contrast, sculptors go beyond illusion and provide actual depth, whether partial in reliefs or complete in freestanding works.

Moreover, the three-dimensional qualities of sculpture make it a plastic art. That is, it can and does change visually, sometimes markedly so, as the viewer's physical position changes. A painting is intended to be seen from a single angle, direction, or perspective, and indeed, it can be viewed only from the particular direction chosen by the painter. In contrast, a freestanding sculpture can be seen from many different angles and looks different from each of those angles. Modern American sculptor Jerry Ward puts it this way:

> In a painting, you are in the hands of the painter. You as the viewer cannot change the perspective, the point of view, or the lighting. This is not the case with sculpture. In effect, sculpture is more interactive than painting. You move, and the sculpture changes. If the light-

ing is changed, the sculpture changes. Put the sculpture in a different environment, and the sculpture changes. You touch it and it responds to reinforce what you see. [1]

Neither Ward nor any other modern sculptor contends that the interactive qualities of sculpture make it somehow better than, more expressive than, or superior to painting. All agree that sculpture and painting are equally expressive and worthy art forms. They are simply different ways of capturing or interpreting the images of the natural world and the human condition.

The Few Who Had Both Opportunity and Means

Another point of agreement among artists, scholars, and art critics is that because sculpture and painting are so different in approach, each usually attracts a different kind of artist. And artists who become masters of both mediums are extremely rare, both in the past and present. In the words of noted art historian H.W. Janson:

Michelangelo's *Moses,* carved for the tomb of Pope Julius II.

There is a vast difference between drawing or painting forms and sculpting them. . . . They require fundamentally different talents and attitudes toward material as well as subject matter. Although a number of artists have been competent in both painting and sculpture, only a handful managed to bridge the gap between them with complete success. [2]

The most renowned of that small group of artists who bridged the gap between sculpture and painting was Michelangelo. In addition to his splendid statues, he executed the

Michelangelo's paintings for the Sistine Chapel include "The Creation of Adam" (center).

single most famous and beloved painting in the world—his rendering of the biblical creation, which adorns the ceiling of the Sistine Chapel of the Vatican in Rome.

Michelangelo worked during the European Renaissance, an era that produced numerous other artistic masters as well. Much has been made in books, museums, films, and so forth about the magnificent sculptures of this period. And equal, if not more, time and space has been devoted to descriptions and praises of the ancient Greek and Roman sculptures that so profoundly influenced the sculptors of the Renaissance.

Yet these were not the only times and places that produced noteworthy sculpted works. Most experts think that at least a few such talented sculptors and other artists existed in Stone Age Europe and Asia and in ancient Egypt and Africa, among other times and places. Indeed, such individuals must have existed in every generation of humans stretching back into the mists of time to the very inception of the species. But most lacked either the opportunity to create, the proper materials, or both. So their genius was never realized and recorded for future generations. But the history of sculpture reveals some of what the fortunate few who enjoyed both the opportunity and the means to create were able to produce, both for themselves and for posterity.

The Earliest Civilizations: The Dawn of Sculpture

Many books written in the nineteenth and twentieth centuries about the history of sculpture begin with the contributions of the ancient Greeks. These same books concentrate almost exclusively on Western, or European-based, peoples and cultures. It is true that the Greeks produced some of the most beautiful and influential sculpted works ever made. It is also true that many of the key developments in the art of sculpture took place in Europe.

However, the Greeks and other early Europeans did not invent sculpture. Nor did Greek sculptors work in a vacuum. In fact, these artists and craftspeople were strongly influenced by sculptors who lived and worked in neighboring, non-Western regions, notably ancient Mesopotamia (now Iraq) and Egypt. Yet these Near Eastern cultures did not invent sculpture either. They, too, inherited certain basic artistic ideas and techniques from earlier peoples. The reality is that human beings were sculpting figurines and other objects tens, or perhaps hundreds, of thousands of years ago during the lengthy era usually referred to as either the Stone Age or prehistoric times.

Indeed, the art of sculpture is so old that no one knows for sure who the first sculptors were or where and when they lived.

What is more certain is that sculpture as an artistic discipline developed slowly but steadily over the course of hundreds of centuries. And each new culture both carried on traditional techniques and added its own distinctive stylistic touches or technical innovations. Examples of prehistoric and ancient sculpture have been found at sites stretching from western Europe and North Africa eastward into the Near East and beyond into India and south-central Asia. Thanks to these surviving artifacts, modern archaeologists and art historians are able roughly to trace the long progression of concepts and techniques that led to and made possible the great flowering of sculpture in ancient Greece.

Stone Age Sculptors

Although the time and place in which the world's first sculptor lived will likely never be known, it is safe to assume that the dawn of sculpture occurred sometime after the advent of tool-making. A crucial milestone in the human saga, tool-making skills emerged at least 2 million years ago. Using tools—consisting at first of simple sticks and stones—the earliest humans began to improve their lives. Some tools were weapons that allowed hunters to kill animals and thereby increase food supplies. Other tools were used to transform animal hides into clothes that provided warmth and protection.

Early humans used still other tools to express their religious beliefs, emotions, and aspirations through artistic expression. Painting and sculpture seem to have been among the earliest artistic mediums. Both had already reached a high level of development by about 28,000 B.C. (thirty thousand years ago). In a cave at Chauvet in southeastern France, for example, modern excavators discovered exquisite wall paintings depicting lions, bears, and other wild animals.

These scraping tools were used in central Europe more than 20,000 years ago.

Chauvet and other Stone Age sites from the same period have also yielded relief sculptures and carved figurines. The sculptors used flint tools to carve images of animals from bone, stone, horn, and ivory. One outstanding example, found in the Vogelherd cave in Germany, is a 2.5 inch (6.4cm) horse carved from mammoth ivory. The figurine dates from about 26,000 B.C. Between one and five thousand years later, another prehistoric artist living in what is now Germany carved a figure of a woman from a small hunk of limestone. Modern archaeologists dubbed the sculpture the "Venus of Willendorf," after the area in which it was found. Other similar figurines of women dating from the same general period have been found in Italy and France. Modern experts suggest that the artists were trying to depict a fertility deity, perhaps a nature goddess who in a sense represented all women. As one expert puts it:

The Venus of Willendorf is one many female figurines made by Stone Age sculptors.

> Generally characterized by large breasts, stomachs, buttocks, [and] thighs . . . these figures represent women in all stages of life: pubescence, pregnancy, childbirth, and the obesity of later life. Only rarely do they have faces . . . although they often show individual touches in their hairstyles and jewelry.[3]

These and other similar discoveries in prehistoric Europe in no way indicate that the artistic skills involved originated in that region. In fact, anthropologists have shown conclusively that the first humans originated in Africa. They then radiated outward into the Near East and points still farther east, as well as northward into Asia Minor (what is now Turkey), the Russian steppes, and Europe. Carved fertility goddesses strikingly similar to the Venus of Willendorf have been found in Russia as well as at Çatalhüyük (chat-al-hoo-YUK), an important early agricultural town in southeastern Asia Minor. Also, a number of

The sculpted heads found in the ruins of prehistoric Jericho were composed of real human skulls with tinted plaster overlaid and shaped to resemble skin and thereby reconstitute the dead person's face. Art experts H.W. Janson and Anthony F. Janson offer the following theory for the motives behind creating sculptures that many people today would view as macabre:

The Jericho heads suggest that some peoples of the [late Stone Age] era believed in a spirit or soul, located in the head, that could survive the death of the body. Thus, it could assert its power over the fortunes of later generations and had to be appeased or controlled. The preserved heads were apparently "spirit traps" designed to keep the spirit in its original dwelling place. They express in visible form the sense of tradition, of family or clan continuity, that sets off the settled life of husbandry from the roving existence of the hunter.

H.W. Janson and Anthony F. Janson, *History of Art*. New York: Abrams, 1997, p. 55.

life-size, sculpted plaster human heads have survived farther south in the ancient Palestinian town of Jericho. These artifacts date from around 8000 B.C., but it is clear that the skills that produced them were much more ancient.

Advances in Mesopotamia

What makes sites like Jericho and Çatalhüyük particularly important in the story of sculpture was that these small, early towns arose in a well-watered region that modern scholars call the Fertile Crescent. It was in this area that agriculture first began. More importantly, sometime between 6000 and 5000 B.C., people from the Fertile Crescent began migrating into nearby Mesopotamia, taking their sculpting skills and traditions with them. And over time their descendants created the world's first large-scale, organized civilization and cities there. For the first time in human history, a society reached a high level of complexity, concentrated population and wealth, and technical sophistication. These advances spurred the rapid development of new artistic techniques.

Early Metal Sculpture

In the medium of sculpture, for instance, emerging metalworking skills allowed sculptors to create figurines, statues, and other objects from copper and bronze as well as from more traditional materials such as stone, wood, and ivory. Copper casting appeared in Mesopotamia at least as early as 3500 B.C. One way to make copper or bronze sculptures was to heat the metal until it was molten, or liquid, and pour it into prepared stone molds. The sculptors then allowed the metal to cool and solidify. The resulting object was solid metal, which made it heavy and expensive to produce.

Mesopotamian sculptors—all of whom were men—also developed a more complex hollow-casting process that produced larger sculptures using less metal. First, a sculptor carved a wooden model of the object he intended to cast later in metal. He covered the model with clay and baked it in a fire or small oven, then removed the wooden core, leaving a hollow mold of hardened clay. In the final step, the sculptor poured liquid copper or bronze into the mold. And when the metal had hardened, he removed the clay, leaving the desired metal object. This was how the famous surviving bronze bust of the early Mesopotamian king Sargon of Akkad was created. The exquisite artifact, now on display in a museum in the Iraqi city of Baghdad, is so skillfully executed that it realistically shows individual locks of hair and even Sargon's mustache.

Meanwhile, Mesopotamian sculptors continued to produce statues and other objects from materials such as wood and stone. Sometimes they combined wood with metal, for instance by applying a layer of bronze to the outer surface of a wooden core. Gold was an especially popular choice for this technique. Modern excavators digging at Ur, an ancient Sumerian city near the shores of the Persian Gulf, discovered a bull's head consisting of a wooden core covered by layers of gold leaf.

Some of the stone sculptures produced in ancient Mesopotamia were freestanding—for example, statues, busts, and animal figurines. The statues usually depicted gods, human rulers, or mythical creatures. The most common kinds of stone employed by local sculptors were alabaster, limestone, and

The famous bronze head of the Akkadian ruler Sargon was made by pouring liquid bronze into a hollow mold.

gypsum. These were chosen because they are relatively soft and easy to carve. One Mesopotamian monarch, Gudea, who ruled the Sumerian city of Lagash from about 2141 to 2122 B.C., ordered sculptors to make numerous stone images of him of various sizes; a number of these technically impressive works have survived intact. The Mesopotamians also created some much larger stone sculptures. Some of the most familiar to modern observers are several enormous, human-headed bulls, each weighing 20 tons (18 metric tons) or more, that the Assyrian kings ordered to be placed at the entrances to their palaces.

The warlike Assyrians, who created in Mesopotamia in the first millennium B.C. one of the largest empires in world history, also excelled at making relief sculptures. Most of these were carved into long panels that decorated the walls of the royal palaces at Nineveh and other Assyrian cities. The sculpted

Huge carved Assyrian bulls with human heads now stand in the Louvre museum in Paris.

PERSIAN ROCK CARVINGS

*L*ater Mesopotamian peoples, including the Persians, were influenced by and carried on the traditions of Assyrian relief sculptures. One of the most famous and visually striking of the relief sculptures created in Mesopotamia after the fall of the Assyrian Empire in the late seventh century B.C. was that on the Behistun Rock, a large stone outcrop located near the village of Bagastana, not far from the ancient metropolis of Babylon. On a cliff face on one side of the rock, the sculptors of the Persian king Darius I (reigned 522–486 B.C.) carved several huge human figures in low relief, along with inscriptions that glorified Darius and his achievements. In the scene of sculpted figures, the king towers over nine of his defeated enemies, who are tied together by ropes around their necks. A tenth captive lies flat on the ground beneath Darius's feet. These sculptures have survived in excellent condition, partly because they were carved high above the ground, where vandals could reach them only with great difficulty.

scenes, carved mostly from gypsum, showed military campaigns and victories and other important achievements of the Assyrian kings. Thus, these works were meant to be political propaganda as well as decoration. Mesopotamian artisans did not know how to show true perspective and depth in their sculptures. To indicate that one figure or object lay behind another, therefore, they carved the more distant one above the closer one.

However, this small drawback does not detract from the often striking amount of detail and the overriding effect of realism achieved in these reliefs. The late, widely respected American art historians Allan Marquand and Arthur L. Frothingham describe the wealth of detail in those Assyrian sculpted panels that showed military campaigns:

The camp is depicted, the grooming of horses, the cooking of rations . . . [religious] offerings on the march. . . . We see all the details of the attack on a walled city—the archers firing from behind skin-covered shields, the soldiers pushing forward a battering ram . . . prisoners being impaled [on pointed sticks] to strike terror [into the enemy ranks], while others are led away. . . . Then follow the submission of the vanquished, the presentation of tribute [valuables acknowledging submission], and the soldiers bringing in the heads of slain enemies to be counted.[4]

Mesopotamian sculptors often attempted to add even more realism by painting their statues and reliefs. Most of the original pigments have worn away over time, leaving the wood, stone, or metal surfaces plain. Tiny surviving traces of these paints indicate that the artisans used black for human hair and beards, white for eyeballs, yellow to indicate gold jewelry, and green for plants and leaves.

Egypt's Distinctive Relief Sculptures

The sculpting techniques that became common in ancient Mesopotamia eventually spread—in some cases rapidly, in others more slowly—to neighboring lands with whom the Mesopotamians periodically communicated and traded. The peoples of these regions, including ancient Egypt, Palestine, Iran, and India, already possessed some basic techniques of sculpture; these skills had spread throughout Asia and Europe during the Stone Age. At some point, local sculptors in each region adopted more advanced ideas from Mesopotamia and combined them with native ones. The result in each case was the development of styles distinctive to that region.

The artisans of ancient Egypt, for example, produced large amounts of sculpture—both reliefs and freestanding statues—in styles that were uniquely Egyptian in character. Like their Mesopotamian counterparts, Egyptian kings, called pharaohs, commissioned large, horizontal panels of sculpted reliefs to commemorate military campaigns. The difference between the Mesopotamian and Egyptian versions was in the details. Egyptian reliefs almost always pictured the king as larger in size than other people, for instance. Likewise by convention, images of gods were larger than those of kings. Also, the human figures in Assyrian reliefs were almost always depicted in true profile, whereas Egyptian sculptors often carved the human face in profile but portrayed the body in a full frontal position, producing the artificial, somewhat disconcerting, but characteristically "Egyptian stance."

Over time, Egyptian artisans developed elaborate step-by-step methods for producing reliefs for palaces, temples, tombs,

The pharaoh Ramses III fights his enemies in this detail from a panel of relief sculptures.

and other buildings. These methods and the sculptures they produced reached their zenith in the New Kingdom, the period roughly encompassing the second half of the second millennium B.C., when Egypt built an empire that included most of Palestine and Syria. The first step in the process was assembling the proper tools. These included copper, bronze, and occasionally stone chisels, saws, and drills. Next, one or more supervisors, perhaps in consultation with the pharaoh, chose the subject and general layout of the relief. This included the number of registers that would be employed. A register was a horizontal panel or band of reliefs or paintings, of which there might be many, one positioned above another on the wall. The lowest register was always seen as the most recent, chronologically speaking.

The next step was for the artisans to cover the wall with a thin layer of plaster and allow it to dry. Onto the plaster they drew rough outlines of people, animals, and objects. Well before the New Kingdom, Egyptian sculptors had learned to use a grid of painted squares as a guide to make it easier to achieve the correct proportions; the plaster and grid lines were later eradicated during the carving process or covered over by paint. Having completed the sketches, which the supervisors approved or corrected, the sculptors got to work with their chisels. After they finished creating the raised reliefs, they adorned them in bright colors in the same manner as Mesopotamian reliefs.

Egyptian Colossi and Other Statues

Egyptian sculptors also turned out many freestanding statues, some made of stone, others of terra-cotta (fired clay), wood, metal, and ivory. These sculpted figures most often portrayed gods, goddesses, or the supposedly semidivine pharaohs, but some depicted members of the royal family, high government officials, and other ordinary people. In the case of statues of humans, with few exceptions the artists attempted to capture some or all of the physical attributes of the subjects. This artis-

*A*mong the many fine relief sculptures created by ancient Egyptian artisans was one dating from the reign of the great warrior-pharaoh Ramses II (reigned ca. 1279–1213 B.C.). Located in a temple complex on the east bank of the Nile near ancient Thebes, the relief commemorated Ramses' victory over another Near Eastern people, the Hittites, at Kadesh in Syria. Following the conventions of Egyptian royal reliefs, the sculptors attempted to tell the story in a straightforward manner so that the people who viewed the work would easily understand the setting, events, and participants of the battle. A carved image of the fortress of Kadesh is plainly visible. Outside the fortress are soldiers from various lands, among them Hittites, Syrians, and Egyptians, each recognizable by their hairstyles and clothing. Prominent among the figures is Ramses, whose image is much larger than those of his own men or the enemy troops. Also larger than the ordinary soldiers but smaller than Ramses is the Hittite king, Muwatallis, who is portrayed fleeing in his chariot. The bodies of Muwatallis's men are falling into a jumbled state of chaos while the more ordered Egyptian troops press on, a clear indication that the Egyptians are defeating their opponents.

tic convention was guided in part by religious beliefs. Many statues were seen as possible receptacles to house the spirits of the dead, who might choose to dwell inside such sculpted images. The general belief was that the more the statue looked like the deceased, the more likely it was that the spirit would choose to enter it.

Although Egyptian statues were sculpted from diverse materials, most of the surviving examples are of stone. In large degree this is because the majority of the wooden ones have rotted away, and most of the metal ones were melted down in late ancient and medieval times. Gay Robins, a noted expert on ancient Egyptian culture and art, describes how one or more sculptors transformed a rectangular block of stone into a realistic freestanding statue:

> Front and back views of the image were sketched out on the front and back of the block, while profile images were drawn on each of the sides. From the [late third millennium B.C.] on, these outlines were probably laid out on a squared grid . . . that ran all the way around the block so as to ensure that all the sketches matched up. Sculptors then cut away the stone on all four sides and the top around the sketched outline until they achieved the rough shape of the statue. As they cut the

The Great Sphinx at Giza, depicting the pharaoh Khafre, is the largest statue ever made in Egypt.

sketch . . . away with the [discarded] stone, they would re-mark important levels and points with lines or dots of paint. Once they had the outline of the statue shaped, they could concentrate on modeling the face and body and executing the details of costume.[5]

If the statue was life-size or smaller, the amount of time and effort required for the sculptor or sculptors was fairly minimal. In contrast, an immense amount of time and energy was required to produce the colossi, or giant statues, commissioned by some of the pharaohs. Among the more famous of these monuments were two stone colossi representing the image of the pharaoh Amenhotep III, who reigned circa 1390 to 1352 B.C.; each is more than 50 feet (15m) high and weighs more than 700 tons (635 metric tons). Incredibly, these impressive creations were dwarfed by some other Egyptian colossi. The pharaoh Ramses II, who reigned circa 1279 to 1213 B.C., had his artisans carve four truly enormous statues of him to grace the front of his great temple at Abu Simbel in southern Egypt. Each of these figures is 72 feet (22m) high. The only statue the Egyptians produced that was larger is the renowned Great Sphinx at Giza, near modern Cairo, which is about 66 feet (20m) high and 240 feet (73m) long. These and other outstanding achievements of the earliest civilizations show that by the time the Greeks began to produce their own famous sculptures, the art of sculpture was already an ancient and venerable one.

2

Greece and Rome:
The Classical Ideal

Many of the sculptures produced by the ancient Greeks and Romans profoundly influenced those produced in later ages in the West. For the most part, the Greeks were artistic innovators; the Romans, in contrast, were largely brilliant imitators who copied Greek styles and incorporated them into the production of sculpture and other art on a vast scale. In this way, Rome preserved and passed on much of the artistic legacy of Greece to later ages and cultures.

The Romans were most impressed and influenced by Greek sculpture produced from the fifth to second centuries B.C. This period included the era that modern scholars call the Classical Age (ca. 500–323 B.C.) and part of the Hellenistic Age (323–30 B.C.). Indeed, Greek sculpture reached its zenith between about 500 and 150 B.C. However, the Greeks had been creating sculpture for many centuries before the Classical Age. A thousand years before, in the Bronze Age (ca. 3000–1100 B.C.), the era in which people used tools and weapons made of bronze, the Minoans and Mycenaeans produced fine sculpted works. The Minoans inhabited the large island of Crete and other nearby islands in the Aegean Sea; they built enormous, complex palace-centers and traded with distant lands, including Egypt. The Mycenaeans, the first

Greek speakers in the region, at first dwelled on the Greek mainland, where they built imposing fortress-citadels made of giant stones. The most famous of these citadels was the one at Mycenae, in southeastern Greece. Later, after these early civilizations disappeared, Greece endured an economic and cultural dark age. Then, in an era that historians call the Archaic Age (ca. 800–500 B.C.), Greek civilization enjoyed a rebirth that included new styles of sculpture and architecture. Later still, the sculptors and other artists of Greece's Classical and Hellenistic ages built and improved on the styles and techniques of the Archaic Age.

One thing that the sculptures of all these Greek ages had in common was the chief motivation behind their creation. Some were produced as nonreligious artistic decoration or as civic works that glorified individual leaders or the governments of various city-states or kingdoms. But the vast bulk of Greek sculpture was created to show respect for and appease the gods.

The fortress-citadel of Mycenae, depicted in this early modern woodcut, thrived in Greece's Bronze Age.

"By far the largest and most important class of Greek sculpture was of a religious character and . . . closely connected with the temple," Allan Marquand and Arthur L. Frothingham point out.

> Within the temple was the image of the divinity. . . . The gods were fashioned in the likeness of man. Sometimes they were of colossal stature or constructed of costly materials. Other [smaller] statues . . . were placed within and without the temple. . . . Besides statues, there were offered to the gods tripods, vases, images of sacred animals . . . jewelry, and other objects of a sculptural character. The sculptor also had much to do with the external decoration of temples [including both reliefs and freestanding works showing interactions between the gods and humans].[6]

Minoan Sculpture

This preoccupation with statues of gods and other images of a religious nature can be seen in many of the surviving examples of Minoan and Mycenaean sculpture. As near as archaeologists can tell, the Minoans produced mainly small figurines that represented goddesses. These images were made mostly from terra-cotta. Sometimes the artisans left the baked clay unadorned, other than applying a bit of paint, whereas at other times they coated the figurines with a shiny glaze made from crushed quartz, a method called faience. One famous example of Minoan glazed terra-cotta is the so-called Snake Goddess, a figurine dating from about 1650 B.C. Standing 12 inches (30cm) high, it depicts a woman, either a priestess or goddess, wearing a long pleated skirt. Her breasts are bare—a style commonly seen in Minoan art—her arms are outstretched, and she holds a snake in each hand.

Minoan sculptors also made decorations for altars and vases from stone, bone, and ivory. Often the styles of these works appear to be based to one degree or another on Mesopotamian and Egyptian versions. Some surviving Minoan vases have low-relief sculptures carved onto their surfaces. Of the stone sculptures, most were made from harder varieties of stone, which often are colorful and have fine textures. These included gypsum, serpentine, obsidian, limestone, and marble. After carving the stone into the desired shape, the artisan used sand to grind the surface and then polished it to a gleaming finish. The most outstanding surviving example is a serpentine drinking vessel carved in the shape of a bull's head, dating from circa 1500 to 1450 B.C. This magnificent work is about 8 inches (20cm) high and features inlays of crystal and seashell.

Minoan sculptors also turned out works made of metals, including copper, bronze, gold, and silver. Most metal items were made by hammering and cutting the metal into the desired shape. But some solid bronze items were cast using a method experts call lost wax. A figurine, for example, was first fashioned in wax. The artisan then encased it in clay, which hardened, and poured molten bronze in through a small hole in the clay. The hot metal melted the wax and displaced it. And when the metal solidified, the clay was removed, exposing the finished figurine.

This Minoan drinking vessel in the shape of a bull was sculpted of marble and gold.

Mycenaean and Archaic Greek Sculpture

It is clear that the mainland Mycenaeans were greatly influenced by Minoan art, including sculpture. Like the Minoans, for instance, the Mycenaeans created many small figurines, apparently mostly for religious purposes. Noted archaeologist and art historian William R. Biers describes the Mycenaean versions:

Carved stone reliefs of lions adorn the famous Lion Gate at Mycenae.

They vary considerably in size, clothing, [and] position of arms . . . from a delicately painted . . . female figurine about 29 cm (11.7 inches) in height to larger, cruder, and fiercer figures. . . . The idols were made on a potter's wheel, with the arms and sometimes the facial features added separately. Most of the larger figures were painted in simple slashes of black glaze.[7]

Other small sculpted figures from Mycenaean sites show less Minoan influence and more influence from Asia Minor and other parts of the Near East. Particularly striking in this respect is an ivory carving dating from roughly 1500 to 1400 B.C. Modern scholars dubbed the work the "Three Deities." The sculptor depicted what appears to be a child, his mother, and his grandmother, all embracing one another. No one knows for sure who these figures are supposed to be, but one theory is that the child might be a god in his infant stage.

In addition, the Mycenaeans produced other forms of sculpture. These included splendid golden funeral masks placed over the faces of deceased kings and queens and low-relief sculptures, also executed in solid gold, on the surfaces of royal drinking cups. Some of the most famous, as well as the largest, Mycenaean sculptures executed in high relief are the carved lions gracing the so-called Lion Gate at Mycenae. The stones from which these beasts were carved, as well as those in the surrounding walls, were so large that Greeks in the later Dark and Archaic ages thought they were built by a mythical race of giants.

The Archaic Age itself witnessed the emergence of large-scale sculpture of a different type. Unlike their Bronze Age counterparts, Archaic Greek sculptors created life-size human figures from stone, called either *kouroi* (young men) or *korai* (maidens). Their style is reminiscent of many Egyptian statues. Such figures had the arms held stiffly at the sides and the left leg placed several inches ahead of the right. The faces and muscles of the chest and arms were at first stylized and featured little detail. But over time the *kouroi* became increasingly detailed and realistic, as exemplified by a surviving example called the Anavysos *kouros*. "The head of this *kouros*," Biers writes,

demonstrates an increased ability [among sculptors] to render anatomy realistically. It has taken on a much more

EARLY GREEK *KOUROI* VS. EGYPTIAN STATUES

Noted art historian William R. Biers points out both similarities and differences between early Greek kouroi *and the Egyptian statues that influenced them.*

The general stance of the figure[s] certainly looks Egyptian at first glance, but the differences are important. The most obvious is the fact that [they are] nude. Nudity would have been impossible in any formal Egyptian context but was taken for granted in Greece, where men regularly exercised nude in the gymnasiums. The figure[s are] also more liberated from the block of stone than similar Egyptian statues. Although the hands are still attached to the thighs in Egyptian fashion, the arms are separate from the body. . . . Similarly, in a typical Egyptian sculpture the weight of the figure rests on the back leg . . . [whereas] the *kouroi* stand firmly on both feet, with the weight evenly distributed.

William R. Biers, *The Archaeology of Greece.* Ithaca, NY: Cornell University Press, 1996, p. 166.

natural shape, with greatly improved detail. The tear ducts, for instance, are now represented. The lips are formed into a shallow smile, the so-called Archaic smile.[8]

Greek Sculpture in the Classical Age

This tendency toward increased realism in Greek sculpture in late Archaic times continued into the early years of the Classical Age, only at a markedly quicker pace. In the course of a mere generation, static, often stiff, and minimally detailed statues and carved reliefs gave way to significantly more detailed and dynamic-looking ones. The Classical sculptures representing humans did not usually look like ordinary people, however. Instead, nearly all carvings of the human figure, whether in relief or freestanding, now featured larger-than-life qualities of beauty, grace, and nobility. This marked the emergence of the so-called Classical ideal, described here by the late art historian Thomas Craven:

> From the mastery of movement and anatomy . . . [Greek] artists proceeded to ideal forms and faces—to the creation of figures, male and female, beyond those produced by nature . . . to marbles which reveal living flesh within the polished surfaces, faces of god-like serenity, women in costumes of infinite grace.[9]

Of the freestanding Classical Greek statues, some of the finest were those that stood in the vast religious sanctuaries of Olympia, where the famous athletic games were held, and Delphi, home of the renowned oracle, a priestess who supposedly conveyed the words of the god Apollo to humans. Some of the statues at these and other sites in Greece stood on pedestals on the ground, while others were mounted on temples and other monumental structures. Some of the finest examples of freestanding statues attached to temples were those gracing the Parthenon, a temple built atop Athens's central hill, the Acropolis, and dedicated to Athena, goddess of war and wisdom. These magnificent figures stood in the open spaces within the structure's two pediments, triangular gables atop the front and back porches. Each pediment contained more than twenty figures and depicted one of the central myths associated with Athena. The Parthenon's front pediment, for example, had a group of twenty-two statues forming a scene from the myth in which the goddess vied with another deity, Poseidon, for possession of Athens.

The Parthenon also featured some of the finest examples of Classical Greek relief sculptures. Literally hundreds of stunning human and animal figures carved in low relief originally formed two friezes, or horizontal bands of sculptures, one beneath the columns on the outside of the temple, the other located high up behind the columns. The outer frieze had ninety-two metopes, or rectangular panels, each containing two or more figures. The western-facing metopes showed the Athenians fighting the Amazons, a legendary race of warrior women. The inner frieze displayed Athenians of all walks of life taking part in a major religious festival.

The first step in creating such sculptures was to make small clay models based on the chief sculptor's design. Once he approved these, he chose the marble blocks out of which the actual statues would be carved. Next, a full-size clay model, consisting of clay covering an inner frame composed of wood or metal, was created for each sculpted figure. Carefully copying these models, the sculptors chipped away layer after layer of marble from the blocks.

This statue of a woman resting on an altar is one of many surviving Classical Greek sculptures.

The man who created the giant statue of Athena that stood inside the Parthenon—the Athenian sculptor Phidias—was born in about 490 B.C., near the dawn of the Classical Age. Almost nothing is known about his early life. Phidias also gained widespread fame for his colossal sculpture of Zeus that sat inside the largest temple in the sacred sanctuary at Olympia; this statue was later chosen as one of the Seven Wonders of the Ancient World. Among Phidias's other renowned works were a large bronze statue of Athena (the *Athena Promachos*), which sat atop the Athenian Acropolis, and a similar statue of the same goddess made for the inhabitants of the Greek island of Lemnos. Phidias was a close friend of the Athenian statesman Pericles. In the late 430s B.C., Pericles' political enemies accused Phidias of stealing some of the gold intended for the Athena image within the Parthenon in an attempt to discredit Pericles. The sculptor was ultimately acquitted. But he decided to leave Athens permanently and died in self-imposed exile in 425 B.C.

Phidias's Colossi

Like the Egyptians, the Classical Greeks occasionally created giant statues. One difference was that most of the Egyptian colossi depicted human kings, whereas all the Greek colossi depicted gods. The three most famous giant sculptures produced in Greece in the Classical Age were all the work of one man—the fifth-century-B.C. Athenian Phidias, later considered the greatest sculptor of the ancient world. One of Phidias's colossi was a huge bronze statue of Athena that stood outside on the summit of the Acropolis. Some ancient sources claim that sailors could see glints of sunlight reflected off the polished metal from miles out at sea.

Phidias also designed a statue of Athena 38 feet (11.6m) high for the cella, or main room, of the Parthenon. This awe-inspiring piece of artwork no longer exists. But a written description of the statue by the second-century-A.D. Greek traveler Pausanias has survived. Pausanias said:

> As you go into the temple, [you can see that] the statue is made of ivory and gold. She [Athena] has a sphinx on the middle of her helmet, and griffins on either side of it. . . . The statue of Athena stands upright in an ankle-length tunic with the head of Medusa [a mythical monster] carved in ivory on her breast[plate]. She [Athena] has a [statue of the goddess] Victory about eight feet high [2.4m] [in one hand] and a spear in her [other] hand, and a shield at her feet.[10]

Phidias's third colossus was a massive statue of Zeus, leader of the Greek gods, that sat on an oversize throne in the Temple

A modern drawing depicts the enormous statue of Athena that once graced the inside of the Parthenon.

of Zeus at Olympia. This work was later named one of the Seven Wonders of the Ancient World.

To make these figures of Athena and Zeus, Phidias and his assistants first fashioned full-size clay replicas. From negative, or recessed, plaster molds made of sections of the replica, the artisans created arms, legs, and other pieces of the finished statue. For example, they placed sheets of gold into the molds they had made of the goddess's dress and used small hammers to beat the soft metal until it conformed to the mold's outlines.

Hellenistic and Roman Sculpture

The Classical ideal in sculpture continued in the Hellenistic Age, which began with the death of the Macedonian Greek conqueror Alexander the Great in 323 B.C. There was an important stylistic modification, however. Before, sculptors had nearly always chosen divine or heroic subjects, which were portrayed in ideal situations and poses. By contrast, in the Hellenistic era Greek society in many areas placed an increased emphasis on the individual person and his or her needs and happiness. Sculptures of ordinary people became much more common, often showing individual quirks and faults. In one surviving example, an old woman is depicted sitting on the ground and holding a wine bottle, her head thrown back in what is clearly a drunken stupor.

Although such realistic sculpted depictions of everyday people were made by the thousands in the Hellenistic Age, the Classical style that emphasized larger-than-life gods and heroes remained popular. The difference was that the sculpted figures became even more realistic and showed more diversity and extremes of human emotion and drama. The culmination of this style was the breathtakingly beautiful frieze of high reliefs adorning the great altar at Pergamum, a Greek city in Asia Minor. This artistic depiction of a group of humans doing battle with a bevy of mythical giants contains seventy-five figures in all. Each is truly an artistic masterpiece, and overall the

figures display an extraordinary range of emotions, including fear, anger, and agony. "Technically, Greek art had never reached such heights," Biers comments. "It was this art that had such influence on the Romans, and through them on the Italian Renaissance."[11]

Indeed, the styles and techniques of Roman sculpture in the late first millennium B.C. and the first centuries of the first millennium A.D. were based largely on those of Greek sculpture at its height. Beginning in the late fourth century B.C., the Romans, who had long viewed themselves as warriors rather than artists, began to import Greek sculptures from time to time. This trickle became a veritable flood in the second and first centuries B.C., when Roman generals looted wagonloads of Greek art to decorate Roman homes and public buildings. In the centuries that followed, Roman artisans adopted Greek sculpting techniques and copied Greek originals; meanwhile, artisans in Greece, which had been conquered by Rome, continued to turn out statues and other sculptures for consumption across the Roman Empire.

Despite the predominance of Greek influence in Roman art, the Romans did manage to develop their own style and voice in one area of sculpture—portraiture. This consisted of

A detail from the great altar of Pergamum, in which Greek sculpture reached its height.

RECONSTRUCTING A LOST MASTERPIECE

The *Ara Pacis* (Altar of Peace) is undoubtedly one of the greatest architectural and sculptural achievements ever produced by the Romans. It was built in Rome's Campus Martius (Field of Mars) and dedicated to Augustus, Rome's first emperor, in January of the year 9 B.C. The altar was U-shaped and featured a staircase leading to the top of a stone platform. Rising from the platform was a marble wall about 30 feet (9m) square and 16 feet (5m) high. The enclosure's walls were decorated with horizontal bands of sculptures containing more than one hundred human figures, including Augustus himself and members of his family. State priests and priestesses periodically performed sacrifices on the altar in the years after it was built. Eventually, following Rome's fall, the structure was dismantled, but pieces of it were rediscovered in the sixteenth century. In the 1930s, a group of archaeologists collected all known pieces of the altar and reconstructed it.

both busts and full-figure statues, some freestanding, others in relief. These works, which reached their height of excellence in the first two centuries A.D., depicted their subjects very realistically. Human faces and sometimes bodies were rendered both accurately and sometimes in rather unflattering detail.

Although the quality of these carved portraits is high, overall the Romans never surpassed the sculptural artistry of the Greeks they had conquered. But the Romans' emulation of Greek art turned out to be a great stroke of luck for future generations. Many lost Greek masterpieces were preserved in Roman copies. And long after Rome's fall in the late fifth century, the rediscovery of the Greco-Roman sculptural heritage became one of the guiding forces of the European Renaissance.

Asia, Oceania, and Africa: Talent from Around the Globe

For many centuries, European societies and the sculptors and other artisans who produced their art arrogantly viewed themselves and their activities as lying at the center of the world. They were blissfully unaware of many of the cultures of central and eastern Asia, later collectively called the Far East, as well as those of the Pacific Ocean region, often called Oceania. Outside of Egypt and other African lands bordering the Mediterranean Sea, the societies of sub-Saharan Africa also long remained unknown to most Europeans.

Many of the ancient societies of the Far East, Oceania, and Africa developed complex, sophisticated social and religious traditions, as well as magnificent works of art, including a wide range of sculptural styles and techniques. In fact, sculpture became the dominant form of artistic expression in much of Africa, the Pacific, and some other areas. And freestanding statues and carved reliefs of considerable complexity and beauty abounded in India, Cambodia, China, Japan, and elsewhere in the Far East.

The Influence of Buddhism on Asian Sculpture

To an even greater degree than in ancient Egypt and Greece, the sculpted works of the Far East were inspired by and based on religious ideas and themes. Several great and popular religions arose in the area, chief among them Buddhism and Hinduism. Indeed, the influence of the Buddha and Buddhism on Far Eastern sculpture and other arts cannot be overstated. Born in India in about 563 B.C., the Buddha was not a divine being but an ordinary man who decided to search for a path to knowledge and truth. He eventually attained what he viewed as true wisdom, or enlightenment. And this supposedly allowed him, or anyone following his philosophy, to control his own life and fate.

Buddhism rapidly spread to other lands, including China, Cambodia, Thailand, Korea, and eventually Japan. The peoples who embraced the Buddha's ideas were frequently inspired

This sculpted Buddhist Wheel of Law was made in Thailand in the ninth century.

to celebrate them in art, including sculpture. At first, it was considered disrespectful to create statues, or icons, showing the Buddha's specific physical form. In this phase of Buddhist sculpture, artisans instead carved objects indirectly associated with the great teacher. These included a Wheel of Law, depicting the great truths the Buddha had discovered; sculptures of the sacred tree beneath which the teacher found enlightenment; and casts of feet and footprints symbolizing the spread of Buddhist ideas far and wide.

By the first century A.D., however, it was no longer forbidden to show images of the Buddha. And in the centuries that followed, peoples across the Far East carved or cast statues of the Buddha, some of them gigantic. In some areas, these images actually came to dominate the art of sculpture. Almost all the sculpted images produced in Thailand in these centuries, for example, were statues of the Buddha. In China, Japan, and other areas of the Far East, Buddhist themes combined with and complemented traditional ones in sculpture and other forms of artistic expression.

Changing Sculptural Traditions in China

The development of Chinese sculpture is a clear example of this commingling of native traditions and Buddhist ones. Well before the appearance of Buddhism in China, the art of sculpture was widely popular there. This was especially true in funerary art, paintings, and sculpted objects placed in or outside tombs to honor the dead and ancient ancestors. A fine surviving example is a storage vessel shaped like a dragon, a mythical creature depicted often in ancient Chinese mythology. Discovered in a tomb at Zhonshan in southern China, the object was cast in bronze and inlaid with streaks of gold and silver. In fact, the early Chinese became highly skilled in bronze-casting methods, including pouring the molten metal into various kinds of molds.

Early Chinese sculptors were just as adept with other materials, however, including wood, ivory, horn, jade, stone,

GREAT ART BECOMES THE VICTIM OF INTOLERANCE

Until recently, the so-called Buddhas of Bamian were among the largest sculpted images in the world. Bamian is located in Afghanistan about 205 miles (330km) northwest of Kabul and was the focus of a great deal of Buddhist activity in the seventh century A.D., when the statues were created. These giants—one standing 180 feet (55m) high, the other 125 feet (38m) high—were carved directly from the face of an immense sandstone cliff. They were originally coated with a mixture of mud and straw, followed by a thin layer of crushed gypsum, and then painted. People around the world were horrified and saddened when in 2001 these ancient treasures were willfully destroyed by members of the Taliban, the ultraconservative Muslims then in control of Afghanistan. The vandals claimed that the Buddhas were pagan idols that demeaned their own religion; however, numerous Muslims in other nations roundly condemned the destruction. Now that the Taliban is no longer in power, there has been some talk of restoring the two colossi. But to date no country or group has raised the necessary funds for such a project.

and especially terra-cotta. The most outstanding example of terra-cotta sculpture in China, and perhaps in the world, is an army of clay warriors sculpted for the tomb of the first emperor of China, Shih Huang Ti (or Qin Shihuangdi), who died in 210 B.C. Among other incredible artistic and technical wonders, the tomb contains more than seven thousand life-size figures of soldiers and horses, probably meant to guard and defend the emperor in the afterlife. As explained by Ann Paludan, an expert on ancient China, these statues were created using a unique combination of assembly line methods and individual craftsmanship:

The figures were made from hollow molds of rough clay split front and back for humans, and left and right for horses. The choice of [separate and distinct] molds was limited, ranging from two [molds] for feet to eight [molds] for heads, but by varying the angles at which the head and limbs were attached, it was possible to produce a wide range of figures. Once assembled and dry, a figure was covered with several layers of very fine clay in which features, such as mouths and eyes, were individually carved and molded. . . . [After firing in an oven] the figures were then painted in the distinctive colors of different army sections. This combination of mass-produced, standard molds with individual modeling and carving made it possible to produce more than 7000 figures so life-like that at first it was believed that they were individual portraits.[12]

This photo shows some of the army of carved warriors from the tomb of China's first emperor.

The Leshan Giant Buddha is the largest sculpted image of the Buddha ever created.

Although Chinese sculptors continued to use terra-cotta, metal, wood, and other materials after the advent of Buddhism, the themes they portrayed in their art began to broaden. Buddhism first appeared in China in the first century A.D., but it did not affect philosophical thought, intellectual pursuits, and the arts significantly until the fifth and sixth centuries. Over time, large numbers of images of the Buddha were carved in bronze, wood, and terra-cotta; these reached their height of technical sophistication and stylistic realism during the T'ang dynasty, lasting from about 618 to 907. However, a number of these works were destroyed in the last years of the T'ang period, when some conservative rulers launched a purge against so-called foreign influences, including Buddhism.

Nevertheless, many sculpted images of the Buddha and other religious icons survived in China. Some were stored in caves. One, the Leshan Giant Buddha, was so big that it could be neither moved nor destroyed. Carved from the side of a cliff and towering to a height of 233 feet (71m), it remains the largest sculpted image of the Buddha in the world. It was said that soon after work began on the statue in the year 713, the government threatened to cut off funding for the project. The chief sculptor, a Buddhist monk, was so distraught that he gouged out his own eyes. The Leshan Buddha was completed by the monk's disciples about ninety years later.

India and Cambodia

Not surprisingly, Buddhist sculptures were also popular in India, the Buddha's native country. And as happened in China, Buddhist themes and styles tended to commingle with and complement, rather than replace, existing non-Buddhist ones. A particularly striking example was what is sometimes called the Greco-Buddhist style of sculpture. In the 320s B.C., the Greek war leader Alexander the Great had invaded western India. Although he had failed to conquer the whole country, he had established permanent towns in the region, particularly in Bactria (what is now northeastern Afghanistan). In nearby Gandhara, then in northern India but now in Pakistan, skilled

Greek and Indian sculptors pooled their resources. They produced many finely crafted busts and statues of the Buddha that showed clear Greek influences, including wavy hair, draped cloaks, sandals, and carved decorations featuring acanthus leaves. Although the Buddha was a teacher rather than a god, Greek sculptors had a strong tradition of carved statues of gods. The result was a subcategory of Indian sculpture that portrayed the Buddha as a man-god, an image that some other Asian peoples later eagerly adopted.

India also had a long-standing tradition of reconciling Hindu religious ideas with Buddhist philosophical doctrines. Hinduism had developed in the area in the first millennium B.C., before the advent of Buddhism. In fact, the Buddha himself started out as a Hindu prince. Hinduism had a pantheon of gods, including Vishnu, the preserver and chief god; Brahma, the creator; and Shiva, the destroyer; along with a set of formal rituals for worshipping them. Many early Hindus viewed Buddhist philosophy as a tool a person could use to become enlightened about the nature of the gods. One result

In this sculpted image from Angkor Wat, demons churn an ocean to extract the liquor of immortality.

of this merging of ideas was a similar merging of Hindu and Buddhist art, including many finely executed low- and high-sculpted reliefs that decorated temples. Some of the figures, often carved from soft sandstone, were Hindu gods and goddesses, while others were representations of the Buddha.

By the tenth century, however, political and religious changes threatened Indian Buddhists. And soon afterward, Hinduism and a newer faith, Islam, prevailed in India, and Buddhism largely disappeared from the country. The triumph of Hinduism is reflected in the grandeur of a cluster of temples erected at Khajuraho in central India around A.D. 1000. Originally there were eighty-five structures in the group. Of the twenty-two that survive, almost all of their exterior surfaces are crammed with relief sculptures carved from the sandstone used to construct the walls. The largest temple, dedicated to Shiva, had more than nine hundred sculpted figures of people and animals.

Another vast Asian temple complex inspired by belief in the Hindu gods is Angkor Wat, built by the kings of the Khmer Empire in the early twelfth century. The Khmer homeland is now part of the modern nation of Cambodia. The main temple in the complex is dedicated to Vishnu and, like the structures at Khajuraho, is decorated with numerous intricate and beautiful carved reliefs. The most famous of these sculptures is the Churning of the Milky Ocean; in highly detailed low relief, it shows ancient Hindu deities creating the divine elixir that would give them immortality.

Japan and the Pacific Region

By the time the temple complexes at Khajuraho and Angkor Wat were erected, Buddhism had already arrived in Japan. And as had been the case in other Asian cultures, Buddhist ideas had a profound effect on Japanese art, including sculpture. Before the appearance of Buddhism in Japan, most sculpture took the form of haniwa, small human figures, animals, boats, and houses modeled in terra-cotta. These were usually placed outside people's tombs, perhaps as symbolic guardians of the dead.

MOVING THE EASTER ISLAND GIANTS

*V*isitors to Easter Island (Rapa Nui) have long wondered how the island's famous giant sculpted heads, called *Moai* each weighing several tons, were moved. The natives lacked metal tools and even the wheel yet they transported these colossi from the quarries where they were carved several miles overland to their final resting places. Experts now believe that rope and timber were their primary tools.

1. Moving *Moai* from Quarry

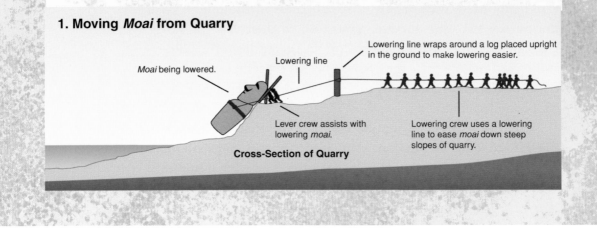

Moai being lowered.

Lowering line

Lowering line wraps around a log placed upright in the ground to make lowering easier.

Lever crew assists with lowering *moai*.

Lowering crew uses a lowering line to ease *moai* down steep slopes of quarry.

Cross-Section of Quarry

With the advent of Buddhism in Japan in the sixth century A.D., the Japanese found a way to reconcile their native Shinto religious beliefs with Buddhist philosophy. At the same time, they began fashioning statues of the Buddha, some of which were huge. In 752, a group of sculptors commissioned by the emperor Shomu unveiled a bronze image of the teacher towering to a height of 52 feet (16m). Located in the new capital of Heijo-Kyo (modern Nara), the statue supposedly used up all existing stores of bronze in the country.

Buddhism did not spread any farther eastward than Japan. So the sculptures made by the native peoples of Oceania were long free from outside influences. These peoples, including the Melanesians, Polynesians, Micronesians, and others, each developed their own distinct styles of art, including sculpture.

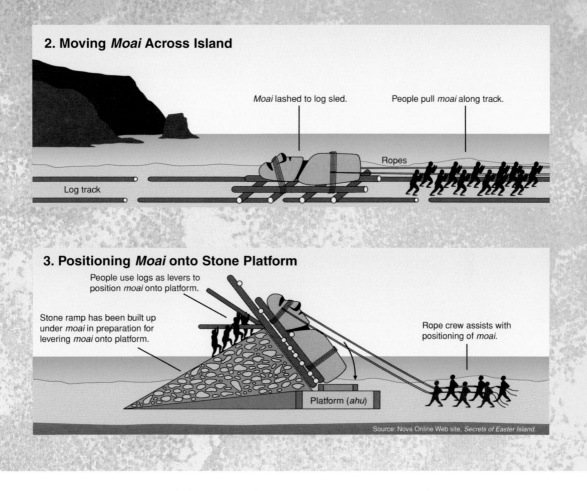

2. Moving *Moai* Across Island

Moai lashed to log sled.

People pull *moai* along track.

Ropes

Log track

3. Positioning *Moai* onto Stone Platform

People use logs as levers to position *moai* onto platform.

Stone ramp has been built up under *moai* in preparation for levering *moai* onto platform.

Rope crew assists with positioning of *moai*.

Platform (*ahu*)

Source: Nova Online Web site, *Secrets of Easter Island.*

Still, certain sculptural themes and styles were common to all. For example, most of the Oceanic sculptures were small figurines that were carved from wood and depicted humans or animals. Also, a large proportion of the human figures were purposely stylized, or representational, rather than realistic. In addition, most of these figures represented deceased ancestors, although some, including a number of surviving examples from Hawaii, depicted gods.

The sculptors of Oceania occasionally produced stone colossi that in size at least rivaled some of those from ancient Egypt. Most of the Pacific versions consisted of immense heads having distorted or exaggerated features. Although such giant artifacts were sculpted in Hawaii, Tahiti, and elsewhere, the most famous examples were those of Easter Island—

referred to as Rapa Nui by the natives—situated in a remote region of the South Pacific. Called *moai*, these imposing sculptures range in height from 6 to 32 feet (2–10m) and were carved from porous volcanic stone. It long remained uncertain what the heads were meant to represent. "Some have argued that they were gods," scholar Chris Scarre points out, "but the interpretation now generally accepted is that they were revered ancestors, deceased elders of the community."[13]

Africa's Sculptural Masterpieces

Some of the many wooden figurines sculpted in ancient Oceania were destroyed by early modern Christian missionaries, who wanted to eliminate what they viewed as pagan idols. But others simply rotted away over time. And that is why only a fraction of the output of the sculptors of the region has survived.

A similar situation arose in Africa, where sculpture was the predominant art form. Some African artisans, particularly in the West African region of Nigeria, used metalworking, including the lost-wax technique. The chief metal employed was brass, an alloy of copper and zinc. But most sculpted artifacts were made of wood. Very few of these wooden sculptures made before the year 1800 have survived. Future discoveries may change present views of early African art, but archaeologists are fairly certain that, outside of ancient Egypt, the area encompassing the Niger River basin in present-day Nigeria had the oldest and most highly developed sculptural traditions in Africa.

The earliest civilization in this region, the Nok culture, prospered between about 500 B.C. and A.D. 200. Nok sculptors produced human and animal figures from wood, brass, and terra-cotta. The human heads were "decorated with an elaborate hairstyle," in the words of one Western observer. "The nostrils, pupils, mouth, and ears are for the most part indicated by a groove, while the lines that describe the facial features . . . are cleanly and precisely carved. The stylized mouth and beard often project from the rest of the face."[14]

This impressive terra-cotta relief was made in the sixth century by Nok sculptors in Nigeria.

Later, the same region was dominated by the Ife culture, which reached its peak between 1200 and 1400. Ife sculptors excelled in creating realistic-looking human heads and other objects from copper and brass. Experts believe that the few surviving examples represent only a small fraction of local art production. For every expensive metal sculpture made, there were likely hundreds of less expensive wooden ones that have long since disintegrated.

The same was almost certainly true for the splendid sculptures produced in the Kingdom of Benin, which controlled much of the Niger River basin from about 1400 to 1900. Many of the sculptures made in this period seem to have been commissioned by officials of the local royal court, which met in a large palace in the capital, Benin City. Evidence also shows that the sculptors were organized into guildlike groups, one for woodworkers, another for metalworkers, and so forth. The members of each group lived and worked in different parts of the city.

All of the Benin sculptures fashioned for the nobility were highly detailed and of exquisite quality, displaying artistic skill on a par with that of the finest artisans of Egypt, Greece, and China. Typical of these African masterpieces is a leopard now on display in the British Museum in London; the sculpture was carved from ivory and festooned with spots consisting of copper inlays. It and other impressive sculpted artifacts from Africa, Asia, and Oceania suggest that the artistic talent required to produce them has always been distributed universally around the globe.

Europe's Renaissance: The Zenith of Order and Symmetry

The European Renaissance witnessed the production of some of the greatest art, including sculpture, in world history. The Renaissance, which for the plastic arts of sculpture and architecture lasted from about 1400 to 1600, was the last phase of Europe's long medieval era, which began with the fall of the western Roman Empire in the late fifth century. The earliest Renaissance masters were Italian, and many of the finest sculptures of the period were created in Italy. However, this momentous flowering of splendid artworks steadily spread to France, Germany, and other European countries. And in the centuries that followed, the style of these works was copied by early modern artisans in statues and other sculptures fashioned for churches and government buildings around the world.

The sculptors and other artists of the European Renaissance were profoundly influenced by the works of their ancient Greek and Roman counterparts. Indeed, in large part the Renaissance, which means "rebirth," was the result of educated Europeans rediscovering the art of Greece and Rome. Yet this rediscovery was not a sudden one. And it would be misleading to view the Renaissance as an abrupt burst of artistic activity that had no immediate precedents or models. The fact is that some aspects of the Greco-Roman cultural heritage were known to Europeans from the earliest centuries of the medieval period. And European architects and sculptors began to incorporate Roman ideas into large-scale buildings and sculptures some three centuries before the advent of the first great Renaissance structures and sculptures.

Romanesque and Gothic Sculpture

Early modern scholars later strove to identify, date, and name these earlier, pre-Renaissance periods of European artistic endeavor. One came to be called the Romanesque because of its connection with ancient Roman art. Art historians variously use the term *Romanesque* either in a general way or a more specific one. In the general sense, Janson and Janson point out, "all of medieval art before 1200 could be called Romanesque insofar as it shows any link with the [Greco-Roman] Mediterranean tradition."[15] In the more specific sense, however, the term *Romanesque* refers to art produced between about 1050 and 1200.

The Romanesque period stands out as a major turning point in the development of European sculpture in pre-Renaissance eras. Before about A.D. 1000, most European sculpture was small-scale, and its diversity of materials and styles was limited. Typical early medieval sculptures consisted of fairly unambitious low reliefs carved onto the walls of churches. There were also small figurines, often depicting Christ's apostles or various saints, carved from wood or ivory or cast from metal. Virtually no large-scale stone sculptures were created in medieval Europe before the year 1000.

The reappearance of such large and more ambitious sculptures was an outgrowth of a rather sudden, widespread, and very vigorous burst of church building that occurred between 1000 and 1100, initiating the Romanesque period proper. One writer of the period, a Christian monk named Raul Glabor, remarked:

> There occurred throughout the world [the European world Glabor knew], especially in Italy and France, a

rebuilding of church basilicas. . . . Each Christian people strove against the others to erect nobler ones. It was as if the whole Earth, having cast off the old by shaking itself, were clothing itself everywhere in the white robe of the church.[16]

In certain ways, these new, substantial churches looked like the public buildings of the late Roman Empire. They had large, heavy blocks of stone and many rounded arches, a Roman trademark—hence the name Romanesque.

One way that Romanesque church builders attempted to make their works nobler was by endowing them with larger, more expressive sculptures than had been seen on the continent in many centuries. The majority of these works were relief figures carved into the capitals, or tops, of pillars and onto

This carved ivory plaque showing a biblical scene survives from sixth-century Italy.

church doors. It was also common to crowd large numbers of carved wooden or stone reliefs into the tympanum, the open space above the outer doors and beneath the large rounded arch that appeared on the front of Romanesque structures. Not surprisingly, the themes of these sculptures were religious, depicting scenes from the Bible or conveying Christian teachings. One of the finest examples was the series of reliefs carved into the tympanum of the Cathedral of St. Lazare in Autun, France, dating from circa 1120 to 1135. These sculptures show Jesus Christ sitting in judgment of the souls of humanity at the time of his prophesied second coming.

Depicted is the magnificent tympanum of the Cathedral of St. Lazare, in Autun, France.

The tympanums, doors, and columns of the churches erected in the next period of medieval European art—the Gothic—also contained numerous human figures carved in wood or stone. However, Gothic sculptures, created mainly between 1200 and 1400, were more highly developed than Romanesque ones in some important ways. First, the Gothic figures were more detailed and realistic. They also tended to be carved in higher relief, so much so in fact that some were essentially freestanding statues hanging on or otherwise attached to doorjambs or pillars. Some outstanding examples are those created between 1145 and 1170 for the great cathedral at Chartres in France. Finally, and perhaps most importantly, Gothic sculptures were more organized, ordered, and thereby more dramatic than any seen since Greco-Roman times. As Janson and Janson put it, it was "as if all the [Romanesque] figures had suddenly come to attention. . . . The dense crowding and frantic movement of Romanesque sculpture have given way to an emphasis on clarity and symmetry."[17]

Florentine Sculptors Lead the Way

These traits—increased realism; the trend toward bigger statues; and a heightened sense of order, symmetry, and drama—all made Renaissance sculpture possible. Another way of putting it is that most Renaissance sculpture was a natural outgrowth of developments in European sculpture during the Romanesque and Gothic periods. The first region of Europe in which these developments coalesced in a major way was Italy, and the first city in Italy that witnessed the birth pangs of Renaissance sculpture was Florence. Located in north-central Italy, by the late 1300s this city had become one of Europe's chief intellectual centers. Florence was also a military and political power that vied with Milan and other strong city-states for dominance of the region. One way the Florentines sought to promote themselves was through expensive civic projects, including the creation of large public buildings and the sculptures and paintings that adorned them.

Under these circumstances, it was only natural that
Florence would both attract gifted sculptors from other cities
and provide a fertile atmosphere for nurturing the talents of
native-born artisans. This was one reason why Florentine
sculptors led the emerging tide of Renaissance sculpture in the
early 1400s. Another was that these artisans concentrated
much of their energy on carving or casting large-scale, freestanding sculptures portraying the human body. This had been
the chief mode of sculpture employed by Greco-Roman sculptors. And the Florentines viewed the Greco-Roman, or classical, approach as superior in its use of realism, dramatic expression, symmetry, and sheer size, as most earlier medieval sculptures had been small-scale.

The first Florentine sculptors to exploit these qualities
with considerable success were Nanni di Banco (ca. 1384–
1421) and Donatello (1386–1466). Both initially worked on
Gothic churches, which were still being built. But a number
of the works they created for these structures carried the art
of sculpture well beyond typical Gothic artistic expression.
For example, between 1410 and 1414 Banco carved four
nearly life-size standing figures—the *Quattro Coronati*—for
a Gothic niche in the facade of Florence's Church of

Orsanmichele. These figures were directly inspired by and captured the style employed by Roman portrait sculptors of the late Roman Empire.

Donatello carried this revival of classical sculptural ideas still further. Also for a niche of the Church of Orsanmichele, he carved a magnificent stone figure of a Christian saint, Mark. It was distinguished from the statues in Banco's quartet partly by its independence. Though almost freestanding, Banco's figures were still attached at their backs to the church's facade. By contrast, the *St. Mark* is completely freestanding—the first large-scale, freestanding stone statue made in Europe after Rome's fall.

THE FIRST GREAT RENAISSANCE SCULPTOR

Donato di Niccolo di Betto Bardi, better known in his own day and to posterity simply as Donatello, is widely regarded as the first great sculptor of the European Renaissance. He was born in Florence in 1386 and received his first sculptural training by apprenticing in a goldsmith's shop. Later, the young Donatello studied with the renowned sculptor Lorenzo Ghiberti, who excelled at producing Gothic statues. Donatello's first true masterworks were his statues of St. Mark and St. George for the outside of the Church of Orsanmichele, both completed in 1415. He also executed statues for the church's bell tower. All of these were directly inspired by late Roman stone portraiture. Donatello also helped pioneer a new form of relief called *schiacciato*, meaning "flattened out," which effectively used low relief to create an illusion of depth. Among Donatello's many bronze statues, one of the finest is his *David*, completed circa 1430, the first large-scale, freestanding nude statue of the Renaissance. Another famous bronze was a statue, popularly called the *Gattamelata*, showing the Venetian nobleman Erasmo da Narmi, on horseback. Donatello's last work before his death in 1466 consisted of a pair of bronze pulpits for a church.

Donatello also pioneered a new form of relief sculpture, a fine example of which, the *St. George*, appears directly below another freestanding statue he executed for the Orsanmichele church. The relief shows St. George in his most renowned exploit—slaying a fierce dragon. The style, which the Greek and Romans had long before mastered to some degree, uses a mixture of high and low relief to achieve an astonishing illusion of depth. "The forms in the front plane," Janson and Janson explain,

> are in very high relief, while those more distant become progressively lower, seemingly immersed in the background of the panel. . . . Behind the figures, the amazing windswept landscape consists entirely of delicate surface modulations that cause the marble to catch light from varying angles. Every tiny ripple becomes endowed with a descriptive power infinitely greater than its real depth, and the chisel, like a painter's brush, becomes a tool for creating shades of light and dark.[18]

Michelangelo: Liberating Bodies from Stone Prisons

The strides made by Banco, Donatello, and other pioneering Florentine sculptors strongly influenced other Italian artisans. And over time, the Italians inspired artisans in France, Germany, and other parts of Europe, making the Renaissance a Europe-wide phenomenon. The most influential and gifted sculptor of the period, and perhaps of all time, was Michelangelo Buonarroti (1475–1564). Born at Arezzo, a few miles southeast of Florence, Michelangelo was raised in Florence and worked off and on there throughout his life. He also did much work in Rome for Pope Julius II and other wealthy patrons.

Although Michelangelo was also a painter and architect of enormous talent, he was trained primarily as a sculptor, and sculpture remained his first love. Part of what moved him as an

The splendid *Pietà* of Michelangelo depicts the crucified Jesus lying in his mother's arms.

artist and made him such a great and innovative sculptor was the unusual way he viewed his work and the subjects he portrayed in stone. He viewed the human body as the supreme object with which sculptors could and should express themselves. To Michelangelo, a marble statue was not simply the end product of some diligent chiseling and carving; instead, it was a human body conceived in the sculptor's mind. That body in a sense already lived inside the raw stone block, and it was the sculptor's job to free it from its stone prison. "In hard and craggy stone," Michelangelo remarked, "the mere removal of the surface gives being to a figure, which ever grows the more the stone is hewn away."[19] This attitude, coupled with his extraordinary talents, gave Michelangelo a palpable intellectual and spiritual connection to the greatest of the ancient Greco-Roman sculptors.

The *Pietà*

The result was a series of sculptures of breathtaking realism, grace, and majesty. The *Pietà*, commissioned for the tomb of a French churchman in 1497, is one of these masterpieces. It shows Jesus Christ's mother, Mary, cradling the dead body of her son following his crucifixion. The noted sixteenth-century Italian painter and biographer Giorgio Vasari, who eventually chronicled Michelangelo's life, was moved to write:

> It would be impossible for any craftsman or sculptor, no matter how brilliant, ever to surpass the grace or design of this work . . . for the *Pietà* [is] a revelation of all the potentialities and force of the art of sculpture. . . . This is notably demonstrated by the body of Christ itself. . . . The lovely expression of the head, [and] the harmony in the joints and attachments of the arms, legs, and trunk . . . are all so wonderful that it is hard to believe that the hand of [a human] artist could have executed [it].[20]

Though Vasari and others were sure that Michelangelo could never surpass himself after creating the *Pietà*, many later observers felt that he did so in his *David*. This remarkable piece of sculpture was commissioned as a symbol of the Florentine republic and carved between 1501 and 1504. The earliest and probably greatest colossus of the Renaissance, it stands 17 feet (5.2m) high and captures the body of the famous biblical character so perfectly that the inert stone seems almost to breathe with life.

The Mannerists

It has often been observed that the head and other upper parts of Michelangelo's *David* are slightly larger in scale than the lower parts of the body. Art historians have advanced two possible explanations for this seemingly strange fact. One is that the statue was originally intended to stand high atop a cathedral in Florence, so the sculptor exaggerated the upper body slightly so it would look more in proportion when viewed from ground level far beneath.

Other experts suggest that Michelangelo exaggerated these features for dramatic emphasis. This technique became part of the mannerist style, or movement, which reached its height between 1520 and 1600. Mannerist sculptures often feature a high degree of complexity, as well as somewhat exaggerated proportions and dramatic, frequently squirming, even physically contorted subjects. In sculpture, mannerism represented the last burst of original creative expression in Europe's Renaissance.

Like earlier Renaissance sculptors, the mannerists worked both in stone and metal. One of the finest and most famous stone works of the period is *The Abduction of the Sabine Woman*, by Giovanni da Bologna (1529–1608), from Flanders who moved to Italy as a young man. The work shows three larger-than-life human figures whose writhing bodies and limbs are intertwined in a dramatic tableau that stunningly captures a feeling of movement.

The most outstanding sculptor of the mannerist phase of the Renaissance, however, worked almost exclusively in metal. He was Benvenuto Cellini, born in Florence in 1500. A colorful individual, Cellini chronicled his own exploits for posterity in an autobiography that has survived. A metalsmith and sculptor of consummate skill, he is best known for his bronze statue of the mythical Greek hero Perseus holding the head of the female monster Medusa, whom he has just slain. The work stands 18 feet (5.5m) high, making it a colossus even taller than Michelangelo's *David.*

The manner in which Cellini created this imposing statue illustrates the techniques Renaissance sculptors used to cast large, heavy, metal figures. First, he gathered large amounts of modeling clay and molded full-size versions of Perseus's body and Medusa's head. These models contained every detail that Cellini desired to create in the finished bronze version.

Giovanni da Bologna's *Abduction of the Sabine Women* beautifully captures a feeling of movement.

AN EXPLOSION ROCKS A SCULPTOR'S WORKSHOP

The noted sculptor Benvenuto Cellini encountered a number of technical problems and accidents while working on his famous bronze statue of Perseus and Medusa. In this passage from his autobiography, he describes one of the more dramatic ones—the explosion of the furnace he used for melting and casting bronze.

*A*ll of a sudden an explosion took place, attended by a tremendous flash of flame, as though a thunderbolt had formed and discharged amongst us. Unwanted and appalling terror astonished everyone, and me more even than the rest. When the din was over and the dazzling light extinguished. . . . I discovered that the cap of the furnace had blown up, and the bronze was bubbling over from its source beneath. So I had the mouths of my mold immediately opened, and at the same time drove in the two plugs which kept back the molten metal. . . . This expedient succeeded, and . . . I fell upon my knees and with all my heart gave thanks to God. After all was over, I turned to a plate of salad . . . and ate with hearty appetite, and drank together with the whole crew.

Benvenuto Cellini, *Autobiography*. New York: Pocket, 1940, p. 475.

Because the clay was very heavy, the sculptor supported it with an iron framework. In his autobiography, Cellini recalled: "[For] my great statue of [Perseus and] Medusa, I covered the iron skeleton with clay, which I modeled like an anatomical subject. . . . This I baked well [in a large oven]."[21]

When the clay was baked hard, Cellini crafted a negative mold of the clay figures. He and his assistants poured wet plaster around the clay in two pieces, one in the front, the other in the back, and when the plaster dried the men removed the clay

Cellini's Lost-Wax Casting Process

1 A clay model is sculpted.

2 Plaster is poured over the clay model. The clay is removed, leaving a mold of the model in the hardened plaster.

3 Liquid wax is poured into the mold.

4 The plaster is removed, leaving a wax version of the original clay model.

5 Plaster is applied to the wax model and placed in a furnace. Melted wax seeps through holes in the plaster.

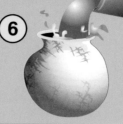

6 Molten bronze is poured into the plaster mold.

7 After the bronze solidifies, the plaster is chipped away, revealing the bronze.

from the plaster molds and cleaned the molds. Into these molds they poured liquid wax. After the wax dried, the men removed the plaster, leaving wax versions of the original clay models. Next, Cellini and his helpers encased the wax in plaster and heated the entire assembly in a big furnace until the wax melted and seeped out through small holes made in the plaster. Finally, they poured molten bronze into the new negative plaster mold they had made. When the bronze solidified, they chipped away the plaster, revealing the finished bronze figures, which they sanded and polished. One of the last great sculptural works of the Renaissance, the *Perseus and Medusa* still stands in Florence. It remains a testament to the brilliance of its maker and other leading Renaissance sculptors in one of the art's finest historical moments.

5

The Early Modern Age: Embracing and Rejecting Realism

For three centuries following the Renaissance, Europe continued to be the center of new trends and styles in the art of sculpture in the Western world. Sculptures of various kinds were made in China, Oceania, Africa, and other parts of the world in this period. However, most of the large-scale patronage of sculptors by governments and nobles, as well as the main focus of art critics and collectors, was in Europe.

The influence of the Renaissance on artists, along with art patrons, critics, and collectors, in the years that followed that epic era was understandably profound. After all, some of the finest and most dramatic artworks, including magnificent stone and bronze sculptures, had been created in the Renaissance. It is not surprising, therefore, that a majority of the art periods and styles that developed between 1600 and 1900 were in a sense offshoots or extensions of the Renaissance. Though in sculpture each of these styles—including the baroque, rococo, and neoclassical—had traits and qualities that distinguished it from the others, all were strongly tied both stylistically and visually to the great works of the Renaissance. Only the last style, or movement, of the period—impressionism—consisted of a radical departure from the others. Impressionist sculptors, like their counterparts in the medium of painting, reacted to, rather than paid homage to, the styles of the past mainly by rejecting the element of overt realism that Renaissance, baroque, and neoclassical artists had embraced.

The Baroque Period and Bernini

The baroque period of art, which roughly spanned the 1600s and early 1700s, produced sculptures that featured the same realistic look and degree of detail as those of the mannerists and other late Renaissance masters. In fact, to the untrained eye the differences between baroque and Renaissance sculpture can be difficult to distinguish. One difference is that baroque sculptors took the human drama portrayed in many Renaissance sculptures to new levels, sometimes even to extremes. On the whole, baroque is sweeping in its drama and emotional feel and very ornate and detailed. These qualities have inspired art historians and critics to describe it as "highly theatrical," or "theater on a grand scale."

Bernini's *Fountain of the Four Rivers*, in Rome's Piazza Navona, was completed in 1651.

Large, grand, and theatrical sculptural displays were extremely expensive to create, so, as had been the case in the Renaissance, the leading baroque sculptors were those who were able to obtain lucrative commissions from kings, nobles, or churches. Thus, the inspiration for the subjects of baroque sculpture came most often from these sources. For example, during the 1600s the Catholic Church was vigorously trying to reassert some of the moral authority it had lost during the Reformation; this was the period of the preceding century when Protestants had broken away from what they viewed as a religious institution mired in corruption. Many baroque sculptures therefore portray religious characters and symbols in ways that venerate or glorify the Catholic Church.

A good example is the *David* created in 1623 by Lorenzo Bernini (1598–1680), the foremost sculptor of Europe's baroque period. As Michelangelo had, Bernini chose a well-known biblical figure. But quite unlike Michelangelo's statue of David, Bernini's version expressed a new point of view and attitude that marked baroque sculpture's departure from the preceding period. In Michelangelo's version, David is clearly the central and sole focus of the work. In contrast, the main focus of Bernini's version—the giant Goliath, whom David is about to fight—is unseen and the sculpted young man merely reacts to that unseen presence. "Bernini's *David* shows us what distinguishes Baroque sculpture from the sculpture of the two preceding centuries," the Jansons point out. This is, they say,

its new, active relationship with the space it inhabits. It rejects self-sufficiency for the illusion of presences or forces that are implied by the behavior of that statue. Because it so often presents an "invisible complement"

BERNINI'S ROMAN FOUNTAINS

Some of the largest, most detailed, and most visually stunning of the many sculptures created in Europe during the baroque phase of sculpture were figures carved or cast for public fountains in Rome. Lorenzo Bernini, the leading sculptor of the age, led the way with his *Triton Fountain* for the Piazza Barberini, a work completed in 1643. He added several dolphins to the base and an imposing image of the Greco-Roman sea god, Triton, high above them. Also in the Piazza Barberini, in 1644 Bernini sculpted a bevy of bees enclosed in a huge seashell for the *Fountain of the Bees,* capturing the coat of arms of the wealthy Barberini family, which had commissioned these fountains. In 1651, Bernini and his assistants finished the magnificent *Fountain of the Four Rivers,* resting in the Piazza Navona. In this work, an obelisk symbolizing a resurgent Catholic Church rises above a group of sculpted figures representing the continents of Africa, Asia, Europe, the Americas, and their major rivers.

(like the Goliath of Bernini's *David*), Baroque sculpture is a tour de force. . . . Such a charging of [empty] space with active energy is, in fact, a key feature of all Baroque art.[22]

Another common technique of the baroque period was to combine the three major visual arts—sculpture, painting, and architecture—in a single artwork. The idea was to create a dazzling, integrated whole in the same way that an opera brings together literature, music, costumes, painted sets, and acting to create a moving spectacle. One of the more outstanding examples was Bernini's *Ecstasy of St. Teresa,* executed between 1647 and 1652. This splendid work consists of an architectural facade, including ornate pillars, an altar-like pedestal, and a roof covered with relief sculptures; a painted panel depicting the vault of heaven in the rear of a niche below the roof; and, in the center of the niche, sculpted figures of St. Teresa and an angel sent by God. As so many other baroque works do, this one employs the talents and diligence of a great artist to make Christian imagery appear glorious and inspirational.

Rococo Sculpture: Whimsy, Fantasy, and Intimacy

The rococo period, most often dated from about 1700 to 1750, followed closely on the baroque stylistically and otherwise. In fact, a number of art historians think of rococo sculpture and other art as the final phase or subdivision of the baroque era. But though the two styles have much in common, they also display some important differences. For one thing, most rococo statues and other sculptures are far less grand than mainstream baroque works. Because rococo sculptures are so often smaller in scale, they are sometimes called miniature baroque. In some cases, more intimate and mundane subjects, such as the family and its members, are portrayed, rather than heroes, saints, and angels. Rococo sculptors also frequently chose whimsical, fantastic subjects, such as satyrs (goat-men) and other mythical creatures, in an attempt to provide humor or escapism.

A typical example of rococo sculpture, and certainly one of the finest, is the *Satyr and Bacchante*, by the age's master of miniature sculptures, Frenchman Claude Michel, better known as Clodion (1738–1814). Only 23 inches (59cm) high, the statue shows a satyr drinking and reveling with a nude woman. Unlike most Renaissance and baroque masters, who either carved stone blocks or cast metal in molds, Clodion created this work using the simpler, more delicate style of modeling terra-cotta by hand or with a few basic tools.

An important branch of rococo sculpture thrived in England, which had produced very few sculptors of any note in earlier centuries. In fact, English rococo sculptors invented a distinct form that artisans in other parts of Europe were

quick to adopt. These statues are usually termed "monuments to genius"; they consist of small or modest-sized carved or cast images of writers, painters, musicians, and other noted cultural figures. A number of English sculptors depicted William Shakespeare, for instance. One of the finest and most famous examples of this branch of rococo sculpture is a statue of George Frideric Handel, the German-born composer who spent much of his life in England. The statue, which shows Handel in an informal pose playing a small harp, was carved by the French sculptor Louis-François Roubillac (1702–1762).

Neoclassicism and Romanticism

The thematic and stylistic essence of the next general period of European sculpture, the neoclassical, is fairly well captured in its name. *Neo* means "new." And *classical* refers to Greco-Roman civilization and its arts. Thus, neoclassical sculptors, who worked in the period roughly spanning the years

AMERICAN SCULPTORS MAKE THEIR MARK

One notable development of the neoclassical phase of European sculpture was an offshoot of the movement that took root in the recently established United States. Several talented young Americans studied in Europe and then returned home and produced imposing neoclassical works on commission. Among the first of these artisans was Horatio Greenough (1805–1852). After studying sculpture in Florence and Rome, in 1843 he received a commission from the U.S. Congress to do a colossal statue of George Washington for the national Capitol. Greenough also executed fine busts of John Adams and John Quincy Adams. Another American neoclassicist, Thomas Crawford (1814–1857), also studied in Rome. He is best known for his figures of Adam and Eve for the Boston Athenaeum and a bronze statue of Beethoven for the Boston Music Hall. In 1882, still another American neoclassicist, John Q.A. Ward (1830–1882) was commissioned to create a large statue of George Washington for the steps of Federal Hall on Wall Street in New York City. Ward also created a number of bronze statues for that city's Central Park; in addition, he founded the National Sculpture Society and served as its first president.

1750–1850 or in some cases somewhat later, sought to revive Greco-Roman themes and styles. They were at first greatly inspired by the discovery in the mid-1700s of the ancient Roman cities of Pompeii and Herculaneum, which had been buried during the eruption of the volcano Mount Vesuvius in A.D. 79. The steady stream of magnificent sculptures unearthed from the buried cities inspired a new generation of artists to try to recapture in an almost literal way the so-called glory of Greece and grandeur of Rome.

The Advent of the Enlightenment

Neoclassicist sculptors and other artists were also guided by the advent of the European Enlightenment, which was itself profoundly influenced by ancient Greek philosophical and political ideas. The Enlightenment was an intellectual movement that swept through Europe and some other parts of the world in the 1700s. Enlightenment thinkers such as England's John Locke, France's Voltaire and Charles de Montesquieu, and Thomas Jefferson in the infant United States, emphasized and championed a number of concepts now seen as modern, progressive, and ennobling of the human spirit. These included the power of human reason, newly discovered scientific facts that revealed humanity's place in the universe, religious toleration, the existence of certain basic natural human rights, and fair, democratic government. The fact that so much of the new rationalism was based on Greek rationalism inspired neoclassicist sculptors, who set a goal of making modern versions of ancient classics.

However, this approach "was not merely a matter of style and subject matter," as Janson and Janson put it. Many sculptors of the era started out poor and obscure and did not enjoy commissions from wealthy patrons. Thus, these artisans "had to find a [relatively cheap] way of creating monumental sculpture in the hope that critical acclaim would establish such works as modern classics and attract buyers."[23] The solution to this problem was the use of inexpensive plaster to make so-called original plasters of the sculptures from plaster molds. These plaster versions were displayed in art exhibitions, and when a someone agreed to buy the work, the sculptor made a stone or bronze version of it.

One of the greatest neoclassical sculptors was an Italian, Antonio Canova (1757–1822), who was the most renowned and sought-after sculptor in the world from the 1790s to his death. A well-known example of his work is an imposing facade for the tomb of Maria Christina, an Austrian noblewoman. The front of the tomb features several life-size

VXORI · OPTIMAE
ALBERTVS

carved human figures, all dressed in Greco-Roman attire, along with a winged youth reminiscent of the Roman deity Cupid. These carved figures appear to be mourning the deceased.

Canova's use of classical themes and models is also illustrated in a number of portraits he did on commission for aristocrats and other high-placed people. The most famous is a statue of the French dictator Napoléon Bonaparte, completed in 1806. The figure, which is larger than life-size, bears a somewhat idealized version of Napoléon's face and head attached to a handsome, muscular, nude body in the style of ancient Greek statues of Apollo and other gods. Napoléon's sister, Pauline Borghese, was so impressed with it that she paid Canova to sculpt a statue of her as a reclining nude Venus, the Roman goddess of love.

Some art historians label Canova and some of his contemporaries as practitioners of romantic as well as neoclassical sculpture. In the medium of sculpture, romanticism was not a separate movement or style, however. Rather, it was a sort of subdivision of neoclassicism motivated by the state of mind or personal tastes of individual artisans. In essence, the romantics were neoclassicists who either chose highly emotional, dramatic themes or combined several different styles from the past in one work.

However one chooses to label its creator, French sculptor Auguste Bartholdi (1834–1904), the most ambitious sculpture of the neoclassical-romantic period was the Statue of Liberty. Its official title is *Liberty Enlightening the World*. Funded by contributions from the people of France, the statue is made of sheets of copper attached to a metal skeleton and stands a whopping 150 feet (46m) high. It was placed on a huge pedestal on a small island in New York Harbor and inaugurated in 1886. This great work, which quickly became a symbol of the United States, depicts a woman wearing an ancient Greco-Roman costume; she stands in a pose similar to that attributed to the Colossus of Rhodes, a giant bronze statue of the sun god Helios erected in the fourth century B.C. on the Greek island of Rhodes.

Auguste Bartholdi's Statue of Liberty remains one of the largest sculpted images in the world.

The Impressionists Reject Realism

In the same years that Bartholdi was creating the Statue of Liberty and other imposing works in the realistic neoclassical style, other European sculptors were rejecting realism and experimenting with daring new forms. These artisans, most often called the impressionists, felt that to be good, sculpture did not need to reproduce all the surface details of a subject. Instead, these artisans attempted to capture, in varying degrees, the mere essence, or an impression, of the person or object they sculpted. Moreover, they felt that such an impression should reveal the inner qualities, beauty, or truth of the subject instead of merely its surface qualities. The leading sculptor of the impressionist movement, France's Auguste Rodin (1840–1917), put it this way:

Rodin's *The Thinker* looks unfinished, as do other examples of impressionist sculpture.

If the artist only reproduces superficial features as photography does, if he copies the lineaments of a face exactly, without reference to character, he deserves no admiration. The resemblance which he ought to obtain is that of the soul.[24]

Because the impressionists revealed the essence of their subjects in a very subjective manner and shunned overt realism, their sculptures have a rough, sketchy look that is often described as "unfinished."

This look was well illustrated in Rodin's first great work, *The Man with the Broken Nose*, a bust created in 1864. He asked a local workman named Bibi to sit for him and made no attempt to idealize the man's face, which was careworn and featured a prominent broken nose. This was in marked contrast to the neoclassicist Canova, who had purposely enhanced Napoléon's features. To Rodin, what many people saw as flaws in Bibi's face were important parts of his character, so he included them, though they appear roughed in rather than finely sculpted.

The same style is evident in Rodin's most famous work, *The Thinker*, completed in 1889. Though he had rejected overt realism in his work, Rodin retained some of the basic ideals of the Renaissance and neoclassical movements. One of these was the conviction that the nude human body is the noblest subject an artist can portray. Rodin later described *The Thinker* as "a naked man, seated on a rock, his fist against his teeth." Yet the features

IMPRESSIONISM'S LEADING WOMAN SCULPTOR

The French impressionist sculptor Auguste Rodin had a major influence on numerous young European sculptors. Among them was Camille Claudel (1864–1943), one of the few women sculptors to make a mark in the art world in the nineteenth century. She began studying with Rodin in his studio at age nineteen and became his mistress. Indeed, her personal feelings for the great master were so strong that her earlier works closely resembled his. Later, however, she found her own voice to some degree in sculptures such as the *Bronze Waltz* (1893) and *Age of Maturity* (1900). Though Claudel was a brilliant sculptor who might have had a long and successful career, she eventually suffered from severe mental illness; this resulted in her destroying some ninety of her works and enduring a long period of confinement in a mental hospital. Claudel's stormy relationship with Rodin was the subject of an acclaimed 1988 film, *Camille Claudel*, starring Isabelle Adjani as Claudel and Gerard Depardieu as Rodin.

of the man portrayed are only sketched in, as if his outer attributes are secondary to his inner thoughts. "He dreams," Rodin said. "The fertile thought slowly elaborates itself within his brain. He is no longer a dreamer, he is a creator."[25]

Another of Rodin's sculptures, the *Monument to Balzac*, a statue of the noted early-nineteenth-century French novelist Honore de Balzac, departs even more from the realism and symmetry of the past than *The Thinker*. The *Balzac* consists almost entirely of a large, shroudlike cloak sculpted in spare detail and tipped at a daring angle, creating a strong asymmetric look. From the upper folds of the cloak protrudes Balzac's rough-hewn face, staring into the distance with an expression of what appears to be discontent.

Rodin's use of diagonal lines in the figure was influenced by a brilliant Italian impressionist, Medardo Rosso (1858–1928). In particular, Rosso's *The Bookmaker* (1894) and *Man Reading* (1895) show sketchy human figures tipped at odd angles. The famous impressionist painters Paul Gauguin and Edgar Degas also experimented with sculptures that consisted mainly of small figurines displaying limited detail and striving to capture the basic character traits of their subjects.

Just as important as the innate qualities of the works created by these and other impressionists was the effect that they had on later generations of sculptors. Most of the styles and movements of the twentieth century departed even further from the realism of the past. Thus, as art critic Joseph Phelan remarks, Rodin, Rosso, and the other impressionists were among "those artists who form a bridge between the Romanticism of the 19th century and the Modernism of the 20th, allowing us to see how we arrived at where we are now."[26]

6

The Twentieth Century: A Fresh New Look at the World

The revolt against realism in the arts that began with the impressionists in the late 1800s continued with renewed vigor in the early decades of the twentieth century. Most of the art movements of that century, including those in which sculptors played a part, rejected literal representations of objects in the natural world. Instead, a new breed of artisans stressed the importance of less tangible elements of the people and things they portrayed. These elements included feelings and emotions, imagery born of the subconscious mind, and subjective or hidden ideas and truths about life. Like the impressionists, therefore, twentieth-century sculptors sought to capture or emphasize the essence of things rather than their surface qualities.

The difference was that most impressionistic works bore a fairly close resemblance to their subjects; someone looking at Rodin's *The Thinker*, for instance, was immediately aware that it represented a naked man sitting on a rock. In contrast, most twentieth-century sculptors went much further. They often distorted the normal images and shapes of the natural world so much that the identities of their subjects were not immediately obvious to average observers.

The art movements and styles in which these daring modern sculptors worked included, among numerous others, cubism, Dadaism, futurism, surrealism, minimalism, and conceptual art. The various movements developed rapidly and often either branched off from one another or overlapped. And artisans working in one movement frequently experimented with ideas and forms from other movements. For these reasons, art historians sometimes differ on what distinguishes one modern style from others. Experts also vary sometimes in their assignment of specific artisans to certain art movements. For example, some accounts describe the popular Italian sculptor Umberto Boccioni (1882–1916) as a futurist, whereas others label him a cubist because futurism developed from cubism.

EXPRESSIONISM AND ERNST BARLACH

Art historians sometimes speak of nearly all the movements of sculpture and other arts of the early twentieth century as "expressionist"; in this general sense, the works produced in these movements were expressions of the artists' inner visions rather than literal representations of nature. However, experts also sometimes use the term *expressionism* to denote a specific art movement or style that emerged mainly in Germany during and after World War I. A leading expressionist sculptor was Ernst Barlach, born in Pinneberg, Germany, in 1870. His early sculptures looked a bit like Gothic statues, except that they had little detail and an impressionistic look. For this reason, he is sometimes described as a "Gothic primitivist." The great turning point in Barlach's life was his army service in World War I, after which he became a staunch pacifist. The pacifist themes he strongly expressed in his sculptures got him into trouble with the militaristic Nazis, who rose to power in Germany in the early 1930s. They confiscated most of his works, calling them "degenerate." Barlach died a social outcast in October 1938.

These technical differences are largely academic and matter only to a handful of art experts and collectors. In fact, average people with no training in art or art history are often unable to tell one contemporary movement or style from another. There has been and remains a tendency for nonacademics to lump most or all of these styles together and give them a convenient general label, such as "abstract" or "avant-garde" (meaning "at the forefront").

But whatever one chooses to call the various kinds of modern sculpture, nearly all examples of it have some fundamental traits in common. As one expert puts it, they all

> investigated new ideas of pictorial language . . . [and] explored the expressive possibilities of materials and techniques not previously used in art. Part of their motivation was to urge people to abandon their convenient way of seeing things and adopt a fresh look at the ever-changing world.[27]

Picasso and Cubism

This attempt to view and interpret the objects of the natural world in previously unexplored ways is well illustrated by the first new art movement of the twentieth century—cubism. Although many sculptors in Europe or other parts of the world adopted this daring new style, it did not originate with them. Cubism was largely invented by an influential modern painter, Spain's Pablo Picasso (1881–1973), one of the giants of twentieth-century art. Picasso's initial inspiration for cubist forms came from his exposure as a young man to carved figurines from sub-Saharan Africa. This marked the first, but certainly not the last, instance of non-European sculptural forms indirectly influencing the development of art in Europe, which was still the center of the art world.

The birth of cubism occurred in the following manner. In 1906, another great modern artist, Henri Matisse (1869–1954), showed Picasso an African sculpture he had found in a Paris antique shop. This spurred Picasso to produce several

paintings, culminating in *Les Demoiselles d'Avignon* (The Young Ladies of Avignon) in 1907. It shows five naked women whose bodies are savagely broken up into angular wedges, as if real women had been dismembered and then pieced back together by a lunatic. But there was method in Picasso's "madness," as Janson and Janson point out:

> Some [of the wedges] look like chunks of solidified space, others like fragments of translucent bodies. They constitute a unique kind of matter, which . . . can no longer be read as an image of the external world. Its world is its own. . . . Picasso's revolutionary "building material" . . . is hard to describe with any precision. The early critics, who saw only the prevalence of sharp edges and angles, dubbed the new style Cubism.[28]

A number of sculptors immediately saw that cubism would readily lend itself to three-dimensional artworks. One of the leading practitioners of this new form of sculpture was Frenchman Raymond Duchamp-Villon (1876–1917). His now famous work, *The Horse*, sculpted in 1914, constitutes a bold attempt to depict an animal in completely abstract terms. The horse's torso and legs consist of a series of bronze coils and rods pieced together. Although the finished sculpture bears little resemblance to a real horse, it captures the essence, dynamic lines, and especially the energy of a horse rearing up on its hind legs.

Futurism: A Hatred for the Past

Cubism gave rise to or strongly influenced other movements in the early-twentieth-century art world. Among the more important and popular, which lasted from about 1910 to the early 1940s, was dubbed futurism by its leading members. One reason for identifying themselves with futurity and modernity was their extreme disdain for past political and artistic ideas and traditions. Several futurists, including Umberto Boccioni, issued manifestos listing their motives and goals. "We will fight with all our might," he declared,

> the fanatical, senseless and snobbish religion of the past, a religion encouraged by the vicious existence of museums. We rebel against that spineless worshipping of old canvases, old statues and old bric-a-brac, against everything which is filthy and worm-ridden and corroded by time. We consider the habitual contempt for everything which is young, new and burning with life to be unjust and even criminal.[29]

Clearly, futurism was driven in large degree by the extreme political and social views of its members as much as it was by the desire to experiment with

Duchamp-Villon's *The Horse* (1914) attempts to depict the inner energy of its subject.

Boccioni's *Unique Forms of Continuity in Space* concentrates on the subject's forward motion.

new art forms. Still, that experimentation was noteworthy in that it tested and pushed beyond the limits established by earlier cubists. Futurist sculptors attempted to express in their works the dynamic, violent qualities of modern life. They especially liked technology and machines, including automobiles and airplanes; they were also fascinated by movement and speed, from a person running to a car racing.

Boccioni strikingly captured the dynamics of movement, for instance, in his *Unique Forms of Continuity in Space*, created in 1913. Ostensibly, it is a bronze statue of a human striding along, with one leg advanced far beyond the other. But though one can make out representations of a head, torso, and legs, they are highly malformed and contorted. The emphasis is on the figure's forward motion, as if the sculptor was trying to make visible the normally invisible aura of energy surrounding moving objects.

Dadaism and Surrealism

Another outgrowth of cubism, an art movement called Dadaism (or more simply Dada), was short-lived but had a lasting impact. During World War I, a number of avant-garde sculptors and painters in Europe and the United States became completely disillusioned with society and humanity. To them, the ravages of the world war made all previous moral, cultural, and artistic values meaningless. Their goal was to use their art to make what was essentially an anti-art statement—that all traditional art was worthless. And they used any and all materials and methods, many of them quite unorthodox, in hopes of shocking people into realizing how far civilization had fallen. For example, one famous example of Dadaist art was to paint a mustache on a copy of Leonardo da Vinci's Renaissance masterpiece, the *Mona Lisa*.

Meanwhile, Dadaist sculptors often turned existing, quite mundane objects into three-dimensional art. The idea was to take such an object, give it a fancy name that usually bore no relation to the object, and declare that said object was a work of art. Because these objects already existed, they became known as readymades. The earliest and chief creator of readymade sculpture was French artisan Marcel Duchamp (1887–1968). One of Duchamp's most famous and controversial works was *Fountain*, produced in 1917. It consisted of a simple porcelain urinal he had purchased in a New York plumbing-supply store. Another example of Duchamp's Dadaist readymades was an ordinary snow shovel, which he renamed *In Advance of the Broken Arm*. Though these and many other examples of Dadaist sculpture were dismissed or ridiculed by the general public, Duchamp and his colleagues in a sense had the last laugh. Many art critics came to accept these works as great art, and in 1999, a version of Duchamp's *Fountain* sold at auction for $1,762,500!

Marcel Duchamp is most famous for his readymade titled *Fountain,* actually a porcelain urinal.

For the most part, Dadaism faded in the early 1920s, and a number of its leading artisans began experimenting with other styles. Duchamp, as well as many non-Dadaist sculptors, were drawn to still another offshoot of cubism—surrealism. The surrealists reacted against the material world, especially the concept of rationalism and the surface qualities of people, animals, and inanimate objects. They stressed instead the unseen and often irrational world of dreams and other aspects of the subconscious. Surrealist painters and sculptors felt that the human imagination must be free to express itself in daring new ways. By exploring beneath the surface of things, they hoped to attain a "truer" state than that of everyday reality. This state would be surreal, or "more real," than normal reality—hence the name of the movement. Surrealism flourished in Europe in the 1920s, 1930s, and 1940s, during which time it spread to Japan, the Caribbean islands, and other parts of the world. Some art historians hold that as an art movement, surrealism ended in the 1940s, while others insist that it continued and remains vigorous in various countries today.

Surrealist Sculpture

One of the leading early surrealist sculptors was a German-born Frenchman, Hans Arp (1887–1966). Beginning in 1935, he turned out a series of sculptures he called the *Human Concretion* series. Modeled in clay or plaster, they consist of smooth-surfaced, abstract masses built up into flowing curves and bulges. Ostensibly, they represent some ill-defined aspect of inner universal truths. These works were extremely influential, and in the decades that followed, numerous sculptors adopted or modified Arp's style.

Meanwhile, other surrealist sculptors developed styles of their own. Picasso entered the movement for a while in the 1930s with works such as *Head of a Woman*, an imaginative conglomeration of metal objects, including a kitchen colander. Strongly influenced by the surrealists, an American sculptor, Alexander Calder (1898–1976), initiated an offshoot style. His works became known as kinetic sculptures because some parts

THE INVENTOR OF THE MOBILE

*A*lexander Calder, known to friends as Sandy Calder, was one of the leading innovators of twentieth-century sculpture. Born in Philadelphia in 1898, he initially became a mechanical engineer. But in 1922, Calder decided to devote himself to art. He studied in New York and then Paris, where he met several leading avant-garde painters and sculptors, including the Dadaist Marcel Duchamp and the surrealist Hans Arp. Calder was immediately drawn to surrealism, but he sought to express its style in new ways. In particular, he used wire and other delicate materials to create collages that he hung on a string so that they floated and drifted with the air currents. Duchamp called them mobiles, a name that stuck. Mobiles subsequently became one of the most popular and versatile of modern art forms. In the 1950s, Calder turned to producing monumental sculptures, including a large work for New York's John F. Kennedy International Airport. He died in 1976 shortly after presenting an important exhibition at the Whitney Museum of American Art in New York City.

A mechanical engineer in his youth, sculptor Alexander Calder created moving collages called mobiles to express surrealism in a new way.

of them moved. The most familiar type is the mobile, which Calder invented and made famous in works such as *Lobster Trap and Fish Tail* (1939).

Post–World War II Sculpture

Beginning in the late 1940s, after the end of the most destructive war in human history, some early-twentieth-century styles of sculpture remained popular, although they often expanded in scope and experimented with new materials and ideas. A number of kinetic sculptors, for instance, began to involve spectators in their works, thereby creating interactive displays. In his *Object with Self-Regulating Composition* (1959), for example, Italian artisan Enzo Mari (born 1932) allowed viewers to manipulate the arrangement of geometric shapes he had enclosed in a glass case. Also, in the pop art craze that began in the United States in the socially and politically turbulent 1960s, various artists updated the concept of Duchamp's readymades by reworking them in imaginative ways. For example, Claes Oldenburg (b. 1929) made giant versions of ordinary objects such as toothpaste tubes and clothespins. And the famous American pop artist Andy Warhol (1928–1987) manipulated Campbell's soup cans and Coca-Cola bottles in various ways.

It was also in the United States in the 1960s that a popular new sculpture movement called minimalism came of age. The minimalists attempted to make an artistic statement using as little (the minimal amount of) detail and emotional expression as possible. Thus, their works tend to be stark and plain and employ simple forms, especially geometric shapes such as full or partial versions of cubes, pyramids, cones, and cylinders. The wide range of materials used includes not only traditional wood, stone, and bronze, but also stainless steel, acrylic glass, and products of modern technology. A stunning example is *Untitled* (1989), by one of the

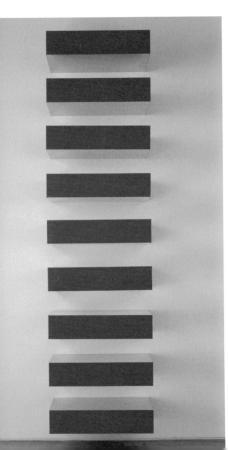

This simple but stunning work by Donald Judd was completed in 1972.

leading minimalists, American Donald Judd (1928–1994). It consists of ten geometric slabs of copper and bright red acrylic glass stacked to form a sort of tower.

Another characteristic of many minimalist sculptures is their tendency toward large size. A closely related style, usually referred to as primary sculpture, often produces works that are so large that they resemble pieces of architecture. Another common characteristic of primary sculpture is that it invites the spectator to walk through it and thereby become one with it. A famous example is *The X* (1967), by Canadian sculptor Ronald Bladen (1918–1988). It consists of a gigantic steel X, 12.5 feet (3.8m) high, that nearly fills an exhibition room of the Corcoran Art Gallery in Washington, D.C. Visitors can walk beneath the lower section. Some primary sculptures are so big that they are literally monuments. One of the most famous is the Vietnam Veterans Memorial, also in Washington, D.C. Designed by Maya Lin (b. 1959), an American of Chinese descent, the black granite sculpture forms a stark triangular shape and is 500 feet (152m) long.

Another popular and influential style of sculpture that emerged in the second half of the twentieth century was part

The Vietnam Veterans Memorial, designed by Maya Lin, is located in Washington, D.C.

of an art movement called conceptual art. It owes much to Dadaism and Duchamp in that it usually deals with everyday objects. A major difference is that conceptual sculptures do not pretend to be something else, as, for instance, when Duchamp labeled a urinal a fountain. Conceptual sculptors accept an object for what it is and in a sense explore the concept of that object, frequently in a multimedia presentation. A famous example is *One and Three Chairs* (1965) by Joseph Kosuth (b. 1945). The work consists of an ordinary wooden folding chair, a photograph of that chair, and a plaque bearing a dictionary definition of a chair.

In contrast, sculptors of one of the last art movements to emerge in the twentieth century, postmodernism, have little or no interest in specific concepts or objects. In fact, by their own admission, their works have little meaning and usually make no political or social statement. Instead, postmodernist sculptors combine a wide, eclectic range of styles and materials to produce nontraditional works that elicit a reaction by spectators. That reaction might be fascination, uneasiness, befuddlement, or outright disgust or rejection. An example is *Washing the Head*, created in 2001 by American sculptor Alison Saar (b. 1956). It shows a naked woman bending over, with a tall stack of pots, pans, and pitchers balanced on her back.

In the Eyes of the Beholder

Clearly, the postmodern, minimalist, surrealist, Dadaist, and other avant-garde sculptures of the modern age are very different stylistically and visually from older, more traditional ones, such as Phidias's statues for the Parthenon, Michelangelo's *David*, or Bartholdi's *Statue of Liberty*. Yet sculptures in all ages and styles have a few basic things in common. First, they are all forms of artistic expression, often of a very passionate kind, by talented artisans. Second, none have ever pleased everyone, no matter when and where they were made and how traditional or nontraditional their style. Like all forms of art, their beauty, meaning, and relevance lies always in the eyes of the individual beholder.

Notes

Introduction: Beyond Illusion: Sculpture as an Interactive Art

1. Jerry Ward, "Sculpture: An Appreciation Primer." www.jerryward.com/about_artist/wood_sculpture/wood_sculpture.html.
2. H.W. Janson and Anthony F. Janson, *History of Art*. New York: Abrams, 1997, pp. 34–35.

Chapter 1: The Earliest Civilizations: The Dawn of Sculpture

3. Enrico Annoscia et al., *Art: A World History*. London: Dorling Kindersley, 1998, p. 21.
4. Allan Marquand and Arthur L. Frothingham, *History of Sculpture*. Whitefish, MT: Kessenger, 2005, pp. 40–41.
5. Gay Robins, *Egyptian Statues*. Buckinghamshire, UK: Shire, 2003, pp. 9–10.

Chapter 2: Greece and Rome: The Classical Ideal

6. Marquand and Frothingham, *History of Sculpture*, p. 72.
7. William R. Biers, *The Archaeology of Greece*. Ithaca, NY: Cornell University Press, 1996, p. 89.
8. Biers, *The Archaeology of Greece*, p. 166.
9. Thomas Craven, *The Pocket Book of Greek Art*. New York: Pocket, 1950, p. 37.

10. Pausanias, *Guide to Greece*, vol. 1. New York: Penguin, 1971, pp. 69–70.
11. Biers, *The Archaeology of Greece*, p. 286.

Chapter 3: Asia, Oceania, and Africa: Talent from Around the Globe

12. Quoted in Chris Scarre, ed., *The Seventy Wonders of the Ancient World*. London: Thames and Hudson, 1999, p. 67.
13. Scarre, *The Seventy Wonders of the Ancient World*, p. 292.
14. Quoted in Annoscia et al., *Art*, p. 184.

Chapter 4: Europe's Renaissance: The Zenith of Order and Symmetry

15. Janson and Janson, *History of Art*, p. 292.
16. Quoted in Leon Bernard and Theodore B. Hodges, eds., *Readings in European History*. New York: Macmillan, 1961, p. 169.
17. Janson and Janson, *History of Art*, p. 344.
18. Janson and Janson, *History of Art*, p. 413.
19. Quoted in J.A. Symonds, *Life of Michelangelo Buonarroti*. Philadelphia: University of Pennsylvania Press, 2002, p. 70.
20. Quoted in Michelangelo Buonarroti, "Early Life: 1475–1504." http://mich

elangelo.com/buon/bio-index2.html?
http://www.michelangelo.com/buon/
bio-early.html.

21. Benvenuto Cellini, *Autobiography*.
New York: Pocket, 1940, p. 442.

Chapter 5: The Early Modern Age: Embracing and Rejecting Realism

22. Janson and Janson, *History of Art*, p. 565.

23. Janson and Janson, *History of Art*, p. 665.

24. Quoted in Robert Genn, ed., "Resource of Art Quotations," The Painter's Keys. www.painterskeys.com

/auth_search.asp?name=auguste%20 rodin.

25. Quoted in Joseph Phelan, "Who Is Rodin's *Thinker*?" www.artcyclopedia.com/feature-2001-08.html.

26. Phelan, "Who Is Rodin's *Thinker*?"

Chapter 6: The Twentieth Century: A Fresh New Look at the World

27. Annoscia et al., *Art*, p. 568.

28. Janson and Janson, *History of Art*, pp. 789–90.

29. Quoted in "Futurism," Wikipedia. http://en.wikipedia.org/wiki/futurism _(art).

For Further Reading

Books

Enrico Annoscia et al., *Art: A World History.* London: Dorling Kindersley, 1998. One of the best general overviews of art history available. Contains a great deal of information on sculpture through the ages.

Carl Bluemel, *Greek Sculptors at Work.* London: Phaidon, 1969. A classic of its kind, this volume provides detailed information about the tools and methods of ancient Greek sculptors and stonemasons.

John Boardman, *Greek Sculpture: The Classical Period, a Handbook.* London: Thames and Hudson, 1985. This information-packed volume is part of the classic series of books by Boardman, one of the leading modern experts on ancient art.

Penelope Curtis, *Sculpture, 1900–1945.* New York: Oxford University Press, 1999. A useful guide to early modern sculpture around the world.

Albert Elser, *Origins of Modern Sculpture: Pioneers and Premises.* New York: George Braziller, 2001. Explains how the distinctive styles of modern sculpture evolved in the late 1800s and early 1900s.

David Franklin, ed., *Leonardo da Vinci, Michelangelo, and the Renaissance in Florence.* New Haven, CT: Yale University Press, 2005. A collection of expert observations of the works of these great artistic masters.

Angel F. Howard et al., *Chinese Sculpture.* New Haven, CT: Yale University Press, 2003. A fine introduction to Chinese sculpture, both past and present, showing that expertise in this art is not confined to Western cultures.

Ian Jenkins, *The Parthenon Frieze.* Austin: University of Texas Press, 1994. A thorough study of the Parthenon's Ionic frieze, with numerous helpful photos and diagrams.

Claudio Merlo, *The History of Art from Ancient to Modern Times.* New York: Peter Bedrick, 2000. A beautifully illustrated general overview of sculpture, painting, and other arts through the ages.

John Mills, *Encyclopedia of Sculpture Techniques.* London: Batsford, 2005. This unique and handsomely mounted book provides a great deal of information on the specific techniques used by sculptors of the past and present.

Gay Robins, *Egyptian Statues.* Buckinghamshire, UK: Shire, 2003. This fine scholarly study by a renowned expert on Egypt discusses the styles, functions, and making of ancient Egyptian statues.

Jane Shuter, *Builders and Craftsmen of Ancient Egypt.* Crystal Lake, IL: Heinemann Library, 1998. A well-written general examination of ancient Egyptian builders and artisans.

Web Sites

African Art, Wikipedia (http://en.wiki pedia.org/wiki/african_art). Part of the online Wikipedia Encyclopedia, this is a useful general overview of the subject, with a good deal of information on African sculpture, a number of photos of sculptures, and several links to related topics.

Art Ages—History of Sculpture (www.art faces.com/artkids/sculpture.htm). An easy-to-read introduction to the major periods and styles of world sculpture.

Contemporary Sculptors, Wikipedia (http://wikipedia.org/wiki/category: contemporary_sculptors). A list of links to short biographies of fifty-one modern sculptors whose works span the period from the 1960s to the present. Each biography is accompanied by links to still more information.

Michelangelo Buonarroti (www.michel angelo.com//buonarroti.html). The home page of an excellent series of Web sites devoted to the life and works of one of the greatest sculptors who ever lived. Contains many stunning photos of his sculptures, paintings, and architectural achievements.

Virtual Sculpture Gallery of Greek and Roman Sculpture (http://man darb.net/virtual_gallery). Click on any one of the links provided here, including "Kouros," "Parthenon," and "Augustus," to see excellent photos or reconstructions of original Greco-Roman sculptures.

Index

Picture Credits

Cover: © Corel Corporation

Archaeological Museum of Heraklion, Crete, Greece, Bildarchiv Steffens/Bridgeman Art Library, 31

© Bettmann/CORBIS, 89, 91

Bridgeman Art Library, 19

CNAC/MNAM/Dist. Reunion des Musees Nationaux/Art Resource, NY, 92

© Conde Nast Archive/CORBIS, 86

Erich Lessing/Art Resource, NY, 15, 16, 20, 23, 32, 45, 46, 57, 78

© Francis G. Mayer/CORBIS, 88

Galleria Borghese, Rome, Italy, Lauros/Giraudon/Bridgeman Art Library, 72

Giraudon/Bridgeman Art Library, 26

Iconica/Getty Images, 93

Louvre, Paris, France, Giraudon/ Bridgeman Art Library, 35

Louvre, Paris, France, Lauros/Giraudon/ Bridgeman Art Library, 75

Maury Aasang, 68

Musee National d'Art Moderne, Centre Pompidou, Paris, France, Peter Willi/Bridgeman Art Library, 87

© North Wind/North Wind Picture Archives, 29, 37

Reunion des Musees Nationaux/Art Resource, NY, 42

© Ruggero Vanni/CORBIS, 39

Scala/Art Resource, NY, 11

Stone/Getty Images, 79

The Art Archive, 71

The Art Archive/Dagli Orti, 63

The Art Archive/Musee du Quai Branly, Paris/Dagli Orti, 53

The Art Archive/Musee Guimet, Paris/Dagli Orti, 48

The Image Bank/Getty, 9

Timothy McCarthy/Art Resource, NY, 60, 66

Vanni/Art Resource, NY, 58, 80

About the Author

Historian and literary scholar Don Nardo is best known for his books for young people about the ancient world, including numerous volumes on the history and culture of ancient Mesopotamia, Egypt, Greece, and Rome. Among these are *Ancient Civilizations, Empires of Mesopotamia, Religion in Ancient Egypt, Greek and Roman Sport, The Ancient Greeks at Home and at Work, The Trial of Socrates*, and *Life of a Roman Slave*. He has also published literary companions to the works of Homer, Sophocles, Euripides, Chaucer, Shakespeare, and Dickens. Mr. Nardo lives with his wife, Christine, in Massachusetts.